DICTIONARY OF AFRO-AMERICAN SLANG

Books by CLARENCE MAJOR

Fiction

NO
All-Night Visitors

Poetry

Swallow the Lake

Anthology

The New Black Poetry

Nonfiction

Dictionary of Afro-American Slang

Dictionary

of

Afro-American

Slang

by CLARENCE MAJOR

International Publishers New York

Library of Congress Card Number: 79-130863

SBN (Cloth) 7178-0268-X; (Paper) 7178-0269-8

Printed in the United States of America

ACKNOWLEDGMENTS

Sheila Silverstone deserves and hereby receives my deep gratitude for helping me do the research—certainly her headaches were as intense as my own; and I wish to thank Corinna Fales, who, during the early stages, did some of the typing; and I am equally grateful to Nan Braymer, the copy-editor of the manuscript for her work and suggestions, to Sharyn Skeeter, Jean Streiff and Max Gundy, who helped with the proofs; and, as always, I remain thankful to James S. Allen not only for his comments but for his vision as a gifted editor.

C.M.

Contents

Introduction

Most other dictionaries hardly need more than an introductory note, since they tend to be self-explanatory; but a dictionary of words seldom found in print, of words with uncertain etymologies, demands an explanation. And at the same time, this sort of situation in itself usually makes such an explanation the object of controversy.

"There are few specifications about slang . . . most people would agree on," wrote Gilbert Seldes, in *The New York Times Book Review* (July 27, 1947). It is, as Seldes points out, instinctive rather than cerebral.

Yet, in the specific case of Afro-American slang it is seldom realized that beneath the novelty or so-called charm of this mode of speech a whole sense of violent unhappiness is in operation. And in connection with this you may ask yourself why do so many apparently well-meaning white folks say with bubbling enthusiasm that black people are geniuses *for* having devised a colorful private way of communicating?

This so-called private vocabulary of black people serves the users as a powerful medium of self-defense against a world demanding participation while at the same time laying a boobytrap-network of rejection and exploitation. I do not mean to suggest that black people are the only people in the United States who are subject to such social misfortune; I am simply saying that our colloquialism provides another ethnic aspect of a long, painful struggle toward human freedom.

It is a language unconsciously designed to pave a way toward positive self-images; though it may seem, in effect, monotonous and certainly no less than tragic, the sociocultural factors at the root of it are revolutionary. In essence, it is a natural attempt to counteract the classic and dreary weight of political and social oppression, and at a very basic level of human experience.

So, the unhappy overtone suggested by the collective presence of these entries, if felt by the reader, should be no surprise. Afro-American slang is created out of the will to survive on black terms.

Most of what has so far been written on this specific area of slang has amounted largely to nonsense. One example: Marcus Hanna Boulware, Professor of Speech at Hampton Institute, suggests in the Forepart to his pamphlet, *Jive and Slang of Students in Negro Colleges* (1947) that slang is a black invention arising principally out of the "jitterbug's limited" vocabulary. But of Negro college students' use of slang Boulware tells us it is because they "want relaxation from their daily grind." I detect something very apologetic in that assessment. It begins from a negative attitude toward the nature of Afro-American slang.

"It is by ignoring the sociological side of the coin that the slick magazines have been able to caricature and patronize the colorful jargon of jazz," correctly states Robert S. Gold in the Introduction to his *A Jazz Lexicon* (1964).

I assert that the speech habits of the most oppressed segment (which is the largest) of the black population in the United States do not spring solely from an inability to handle acceptable forms of spoken English nor mainly from the limitations caused by the particular stock of words known to the speaker.

Black slang stems more precisely from a somewhat disseminated rejection of the life-styles, social patterns, and thinking in general of the Euro-American sensibility. The rejection is necessarily diffused because it is impossible for any combination of ethnic groups to endure the kind of close sociocultural contact (despite the well-known inequity) endured by black and white in North America without showing the effects of the usual exchange and conflict.

And though this is not the place for a discussion of it, even a casual investigation into any similar historical situation should reveal, as Wilhelm Reich has pointed out, that a subculture always has a proportionately *larger impact* upon a dominant culture, rather than vice versa.

Therefore, if we open our eyes, our ears, our minds in approaching American slang in general we will soon come to understand that it is largely *black* American slang—in origin. And though I do not make the claim that all the entries here first came from the mouths of black people Reich's theory supports such an argument. This is a book of the words and phrases used by black people irrespective of their origin. I say this in an effort to preclude any *honest* confusion (and possibly some *expected* offense) some people may feel when coming upon words listed here they will immediately recognize to be in general usage.

Anyway, in the original situation the slaveholder not only imitated (for kicks and to slander) the slave's speech, it was in his Great American Tradition to even paint his pale face black and before a white audience (presumably to entertain it) put himself through a series of shenanigans, trying to *act* like what, in his mind, he conceived a black person to be. And of course today we still get the pranks and the trickery and the slander, the whole show—but in a more subtle way. Yet it seems that all this time the imitator has had no idea that he himself has been the real joke. To *add* to the confusion those imitated often turned around and imitated the imitators imitating them.

The people who create and cultivate and use a code language have a need for secrecy. This is true, in addition to its function as self-defense, and a diffused way of rejecting a system of logic and a history of values which are primarily racist. And racism, unlike group identity or ethnic pride, has never been—not even for its practitioners—in any way a healthy activity. It begins from the narrow and deadly premise of fear and dislocated self-esteem. There is a certain curious but good kind of security generated from the quality known as group identity and, certainly, a distinct and lively sort of life-energy stemming from ethnic pride. They are human values which may be (more often than not) valuable in terms leading to a means by which people different from one another—historically, culturally, racially—may experience *in*directly the richness (if it exists!) of a whole *other* way of life and possibly, in the act, deepen and enrich the inlets of their own souls. But it is the pattern of racism (as we all, by now, well know) which is implicit in too many white values that, in its impetus, Afro-American slang attempts to confront and ultimately to reject.

Sometimes you can identify one who has spent some time in prison from the *way* one talks. It's not unusual for such a person to speak softly but especially out the *side* of his or her mouth. If heads are supposed to be facing forward and nobody's supposed to be talking then you speak from the side of your mouth. And with a minimum of lip movement, and quietly; and if you have to do it a long time it becomes a habit. So, the need to communicate when the need strikes coupled with the need (imposed) for secrecy creates the particular characteristic.

I mention this both as a parable of the historical plight of black people in general and in particular to remind the reader of the horror of the disproportionate number of black men who have been subjected to imprisonment and died frequently at the hands of white "law" in and out of the electric chair. And this also brings me to one of the areas from which slang has grown—an area some refer to as the underworld.

Prison slang, the jargon arising out of the drug scene, prostitute and pimp parlance, the gambling and numbers racket lingo, all overlap and, for the same unhappy reasons I've already mentioned, have been and continue to be a large part of the black experience.

Yet more than any other aspect of this experience the language of the black musician has had the greatest total effect on the informal language Americans speak. From the moment the black musician broke with the Negro Church he became a sinner-man, who, in Afro-American folklore is as *in*famous as the preacher is famous! But being a sinner-man did not always mean that the black musician had broken completely with the business of worshipping a white god-image. However, if anybody black broke first into a new vision it was this man, who, often (at least in symbol and *too* often in actuality) could not be distinguished from the black convict on the chain gang. In a very large sense, he is the same black man who continues to die, always with great ceremony, in the hands of the law.

The sinner-man-black musician maintains a very large and intense place in the total American psyche. And naturally his need for secrecy was always tremendous. Today the influence of his secret and rebellious way of communicating continues not only to wedge itself deeply into the sensibility of black folks but also it has become more than ever an "extension" of the young white person's *conscious* communication apparatus.

So, when bright white kids become disillusioned—suddenly discovering that they have been nourished on lies—and absorb (in larger doses than ever before) the underground language of black America, both as a defense mechanism and as a signal of alliance, it proves that the spirit of revolution continues (as always) to be an intensely real force in the North American experience. But— the *important difference* is: these young whites speak the code language of oppressed black people *without* the old smirk intrinsic in the attitude of their white forefathers and mothers.

We already know that the most original and revolutionary art form in North America, The Technology Society, has been black music. And out of the life-styles of the people who make it comes the vernacular that has made possible certain functional concepts —such as *bad* meaning *good; hard* having a positive connotation; *kill* to mean: affect strongly, to fascinate; *love letter* to mean: a bullet; and *murder* to express approval of something excellent. These concepts are all new in the Euro-American experience.

The sinner-man-black musician, unwilling and possibly *un*able to attain salvation through or to make peace with the worship of a white god-image *had* (in order to achieve and maintain his own chosen style of sanity) to turn *bad* into *good* and begin to change the negative definition of blackness.

So to call this language an *aberration* is simply another kind of insult.

The vocabulary of a people never gives the total picture of the means they have for communicating. It is true, black people in the United States use English, but gesture and nuance, inflection and innuendo, the entire spirit of the black experience itself, are just as much a part of the cultural basis of Afro-American slang as the collective sense of energy given by the words themselves.

Some of the definitions I give the words and phrases I am sure will puzzle many people. It is to be expected, particularly because the evolution of this mode of speech defies linguistic interpretation —so far. If, for example, I have characterized a phrase like "O-bop-she-bam" as "existential" it is my own attempt to define as closely as I can what no one else can define any closer. The crux of many slang expressions is submerged at an unconscious level that hasn't been penetrated by logic. And the mystery at the absolute root of *any* word in the world doesn't help matters. The origin of speech itself as far as anyone can guess is forever lost beneath the elusive fabric of whatever it is that causes human beings to *move* beyond their most basic functions. One theory: the monogenesis of speech is the supposition that all languages had the same kind of beginning. And it may be, as some people think, connected with the origin of symbolism and magic. Even the Biblical personality, Adam, from the very start, finds it necessary to *name* things.

In any case, the speech apparatus (lips, teeth, tongue, hard and soft palate, nose, glottal and the larynx cords), plus the local magic beneath spoken words, has more than a little to do with the character of any word but especially any slang term used by a black speaker. And in a dictionary those qualities cannot be demonstrated successfully. So in approaching a work of this nature one should remember what is necessarily absent.

But to get back to where I was: I use the word "existential" in one way only: to stand for my belief that there is no meaning in life except that which is imposed upon it. We are social animals.

The insertion of dates following many of the entries refers generally to the time in which the word or phrase was most popular. And this information is not the result of guess-work: it has been researched as carefully as it can possibly be done. Also, where dates are not given the time of origin or of popularity could not be established.

Some people may ask about the jargon of the black agricultural and industrial workers. And though users of this book will find here terms from those areas of the black experience, for reasons already suggested, their number is automatically small. It has to do, not only with the fact that slang is an outlaw tongue, but also with the fact that quite a large number—though not all—slang expressions used by, say, southern Negroes twenty, thirty years ago or even today, tend to remain regional and therefore come less to the attention of a researcher than a geographical scattering of urban terms taken into the mainstream and popularized by all forms of media.

But no one should ever think The People possess not the spirit of revolution: because historically The People have proven they do by from time to time (like in a cycle) nearly wrecking the entire nation and always in a desperate attempt to advance the social nature of humanity. Yet the instigation seems always to come from the outlaw or renegade. And he is not a spirit separate from the sinner-man-black musician.

I have gathered these words not only from a scattering of printed sources but from the reliability of my own ethnic experience. And the experience of others.

While doing research for this work I soon realized that it could easily take anybody at least half a life time to come close to producing a definitive work on Afro-American slang. So definitive this dictionary is not, though I hope it may help pave the way toward such a project.

Most scholars who have addressed themselves to this relatively untouched area of the study of language have been for the most part too far removed from the black community's sensibilities and speech habits.

In any case, the few works that have been attempted have all been thinner and sketchier than this present one.

Also, it is worth noting that American slang dictionaries containing entries cited as having originated in black communities frequently give incorrect definitions.

One final thing: I have taken the liberty of including nicknames because I feel that the renaming of people stems from the same need that inspires the renaming of both things and ideas.

April 14, 1970   —CLARENCE MAJOR

DICTIONARY OF AFRO-AMERICAN SLANG

A

A: yes, correct, right.

Absofuckinglutely: without doubt.

Ace: one dollar; one's best friend; a first-rate person; one's lover.

Ace-deuce: (1940's) three.

Action: the vitality or force of a situation, plan, or proposition; excitement; gambling; sexual intercourse; music.

Actor: a faker.

A.D.: drug addict (reversed to avoid confusion with D.A.).

African dominoes: a form of dice-playing originated in New Orleans.

Afro: a "natural" hair style that became popular among Afro-Americans in the early 1960's. The hair is allowed to grow long and is left woolly.

After hours: a term jazzmen use to refer to those times away from public places when they can play without restrictions or inhibitions; very private social gatherings in the wee hours of the morning.

A.G.: the Attorney General.

A-head: a heavy user of amphetamines.

Ain't coming: (1940's) statement of refusal.

Air-bags: (1940's) human lungs.

Air out: to go for a walk.

Alabama: a person from that state.

Alarm clock: (1940's) a college professor (Southern Negro college use).

Ali shuffle: Muhammad Ali's footwork while boxing.

Alley: corridor in a hospital.

Alley rat: a demoralized, corrupt, thieving person.

Alley tidde: a down-to-earth way of playing the violin.

Alligator: (1930's) term used by black jazzmen, particularly in New Orleans, referring to white jazz musicians, jive people or jitterbugs.

Alligator-bait: (1940's) a Negro in or from Florida.

All-originals scene: an all-black affair.

All reet: variant pronunciation of "all right."

Ambulance chaser: a crooked lawyer who patrols the streets in search of accidents and their victims as clients.

Ankle: (1940's) to walk.

Anxious: (1940's) a fine state of affairs; anything good.

Any (get, got, etc.): refers to sexual activity, especially sexual intercourse.

Anywhere: to possess drugs, *example,* "Are you anywhere?"

Apollo play: (1940's) the planet earth.

Apron: a woman; a wife; a bartender.

Are (your) boots laced?: (1940's) inquiry as to whether or not one understands whatever is in question.

Armstrong: a very high note or a series of them, especially on a trumpet (from *Louis Armstrong*).

Arrive: (1930's) newly informed.

Ass: one's self or a dumb person; "your ass" means the end or destruction of the person referred to.

Assed: (used to give emphasis) bad-assed, high-assed, tight-assed, etc.

Ass peddler: one who sells him or herself sexually.

Attic: (1940's) the human head.

Aunt: an old homosexual.

Auntjamimablack: very black psychologically.

Aunt Jane: female Uncle Tom.

Avenue-tank: (1940's) the double-decker style public transportation bus on the New York City 5th Avenue route.

Ax, axe: any musical instrument but usually a saxophone.
Axle grease: any stiff pomade for the hair.

B

B: (1950's) benzedrine.

Baby: term of address for one's lover or spouse but also a word used in general, irrespective of the sexual identity or personal or social relationship.

Baby-kisser: (1940's) a politician.

Back: the musical accompaniment given a jazzman doing a solo.

Back alley: any popular street in a rundown, disreputable area.

Back beat: in jazz, rhythmic accent of a secondary nature; (1940's) one's heart movement.

Backcap: (1940's) a sharp reply—associated with *The Dozens* (which, see).

Back-door man: a married woman's lover, who is, incidentally, a legendary figure in blues numbers.

Back, from way: having been a long while in existence or of amazing time-tested skill.

Back-gate parlor: (1940's) death in prison.

Back off: a command to stop intimidating or teasing someone.

Bad: a simple reversal of the white standard, the very best.

Bad eye: a threatening glance.

Bad mouth: malicious gossip.

Bad news: an unpleasant person, place or thing.

Bad nigger: a black person who refuses to be meek or who rejects the social terms of poverty and oppression the culture designs for him.

Bad talk: revolutionary or radical ideas.

Bag: one's disposition, mood, behavior, life-style, vocation, hobby, interests; a social milieu or clique.

Bagpipe: (1940's) a vacuum cleaner.

Bale of straw: a white, usually blond female.

Ball: to have social or sexual fun or both.

Ball and chain: one's sweetheart or wife.

Balling the Jack: Negro dance accompanied by lusty handclapping and chants; to go; to work swiftly.

Balloon room: (1940's) a place where marijuana is smoked.

Ballroom without a parachute: (1940's) marijuana den where no marijuana is available.

Balls: testicles.

Bam: (from *bambita*) amphetamine.

Banana: an attractive light-skinned Afro-American female.

Band: a woman.

Band man: a jazzman who functions better with a group than as a soloist.

Bang: an injection of narcotics or sniff of cocaine; also sex or any excitement.

Banjo: musical instrument slaves brought from West Africa, used frequently in social and religious gatherings.

Bank: (1940's) toilet.

Banta issue: (1940's) pretty girls.

Bantam: a young woman.

Banter play built on a coke frame: (1940's) an attractive young woman.

Barbecue, Bar-B-Q: an attractive female as an object for oral sex.

Barbecued ribs: roasted spareribs.

Barge: (1940's) to jump.

Bark: (1940's) human skin.

Barkers: (1940's) shoes.

Barrelhouse: a cheap saloon; unpretentious rough music played in such a place, hot music; a syncopated, seductive style of piano-playing.

Barrel punishment: to place a prisoner over a barrel and viciously beat him, sometimes to death.

Bary: baritone saxophone.

Basers: responding line sung by a gospel group.

Basket: the penis and groin (homosexual use); stomach.

Bat: (1940's) an old woman interested in young men.

Battle: in jazz, musical competition between instrumentalists; (1940's) an unattractive girl.

B.C.: birth control pills.

B.D.A.C.: Bureau of Drug Abuse Control.

Beam: (1940's) to look.

Bean: (1940's) the sun.

Bear: (1930's-40's) unpleasant life style; an ugly woman.

Beard: (1950's) intellectual or far-out person.

Bear down: play with great emotional impact.

Beast: the white man; white people.

Beat: accent or stress in musical forms like jazz, and rhythm and blues; highly developed rhythm that has nothing to do with 2/4 or 4/4 or 6/8 time and is unlimited as to number of beats in a bar.

Beat (one's) chops: (1940's) to talk.

Beater: (1940's) money.

Beat for the yolk: (1940's) short of cash.

Beat out some licks: drum on drums.

Beat (one's) skin: (1940's) clap hands, applaud.

Beat the dummy (the meat): male act of masturbating.

Beat the rocks: (1940's) to walk on the sidewalk.

Beat to the socks: (1930's-40's) weariness.

Beat up: (1940's-50's) dilapidated, disheveled.

Bebop: Jazz radical form replaced by "Bop." It employs the intricacies of African rhythms combined with some of the complexities of European and American harmony. Originally an onomatopoeic word applied to the music of Charlie Parker, Kenny Clarke, Dizzy Gillespie, Bud Powell and Thelonious Monk.

Bebop glasses: (1940's) fashionable thick-framed dark eyeglasses or "shades" made popular by jazzmen.

Bebop Santa: hero of a song done as a take-off on the "Night Before Christmas."

Bedbug: a pullman porter.

Bedhouse: a whorehouse.

Bee: an idea.

Before Abe: (1940's) anytime prior to January 1, 1863, the official day of "Emancipation" of slaves in the United States.

Behind: afterward; that which follows.

Beige: (rare) a light-skinned Negro.

Bell: notoriety attaching to one's name or position.

Bells: short for wedding bells; an expression of approval.

Belly fiddle: guitar.

Belly habit: gnawing withdrawal stomach pains from the use of physically addictive drugs.

Bend: in jazz, to manipulate the lips to achieve a slight upward or downward variation pitch on bass; to slur a note; also called "scooping pitch."

Bend (one's) ear: to tell someone something; to whisper some message to a person.

Bender: (1940's) the human arm.

Benjamin (Benny): (1940's) an overcoat.

Benny: an overcoat; benzadrine inhaler.

Be's: shares the human condition; exists, is; *example*, "Things just be's that way."

Bible: (1940's) the truth.

Biddie: (1940's) an attractive little girl or small old woman.

Big Apple: any big northern city but especially New York, term originated among widely traveled jazzmen.

Big band: any group of musicians composed of from 14 to 20 persons.

Big bit: an extremely long, unjust prison term.

Bigger Thomas: character in Richard Wright's novel, *Native Son:* a bad nigger; see *Bad nigger.*

Big Red with the Long Green Stem: (1940's) Seventh Avenue in New York City.

Big shot: (1940's) an important person.

Big Timer: one who flaunts himself or his money or both; often a phrase used mockingly for a square or naive person.

Big Wind (or Windy): (1940's Chicago) the phrase refers to the mighty winds that sweep in on the city from Lake Michigan.

Bill: one-dollar bill.

Bip bam, thank you ma'am: descriptive phrase expressing gratitude to a woman after lovemaking, from a popular song.

Bird: Charlie Parker, the most influential jazz innovator, generally regarded as one of the greatest, perhaps the greatest, instrumentalist in American music; see *Yardbird*.

Birdie: like the sound of a bird; in jazz, a "grace" note.

Birdland: a famous nightclub in New York City, named for Charlie Parker; a life style with after-hours connotations.

Birdwood: (1940's) marijuana.

Biscuit: (1940's) the human skull or a bed pillow.

Bit: a prison sentence; personality trait; one's attitude.

Bitch: any difficult or formidable situation or person; a mean, flaunting homosexual.

Bitter mouth: (1940's) cynical or mean talk.

Black: (1940's) night.

Black beauties: biphetamine capsules.

Black Boogaloo: a rhythm, a dance, the feeling of blackness.

Black Bottom: (1920's-30's) the area where the "nitty-gritty" black population of any town or city resides; a popular dance among black people.

Black 360 degrees: profoundly black in a psychological sense.

Black gunion: a very strong, gummy grade of marijuana.

Black justice: self-determination.

Black out: (1940's) a very dark complexioned person.

Black pimp: (1940's) a telephone operating free of charge on a party line (Southern Negro college use).

Blackplate: backbone and dumplings, baked grits, scrambled pork brains, chitlins and corn bread, cracklin biscuits, fried catfish, fried tripe, etc.; see *Soul food*.

Black stuff: opium.

Blade: a knife, especially a switchblade, carried as a weapon.

Blank: any non-narcotic powder sold as a drug.

Blanshed: to be ruined.

Blast: to play a musical instrument without restraint; to smoke marijuana, especially in a group—a "blast party."

Blewy, blooey: (obscure) in jazz, an out-of-place note.

Blind: to be uncircumcised (largely in homosexual use).

Blinders: (1940's) eyes, or eyelids.

Blindfolded lady with the scales: (1940's) the legal system or a court building.

Blip: (1930's) anything inscrutable or at least strange; a nickel.

Blockbuster: barbiturates, usually Nembutal; see *Yellow jacket*.

Blood: one black person to another; wine.

Blood brother: see *Blood*.

Blow: (1920's) originally carried a jazz connotation but came to mean any "performance"—a writer, for example, "blows" a typewriter; one "blows" grass; also, to leave; also, to lose something; *example*, "She blew her job."

Blow a gut: explode with laughter.

Blow (one's) ass off: (1940's) to make superlative music.

Blow black: (1960's) to talk or write along the lines of black consciousness.

Blow change: (1960's) to think, talk, write or play music along the lines of revolutionary principles.

Blow (someone) down: (1930's) to win in a musical competition, a battle between saxes, for example.

Blower: (1940's) handkerchief; (1950's) a soloist.

Blow, Gabriel, Blow: refers to an American folktale that grew out of an incident involving a Methodist preacher, his congregation, and a small black boy. During a sermon concerning the angel Gabriel, the preacher called out, "Blow, Gabriel, blow" and, by prearrangement, the boy, hidden from the congregation, began to blow a trumpet. The simpleminded white folks fell to the ground begging for mercy, sure that Judgement Day was upon them.

Blow gage (gauge): to smoke pot.

Blowing room: (1950's) time allowed jazzmen to improvise during recording sessions or in concert.

Blowing session: (1950's) a jazz session where improvisation is the orientation.

Blowjob: oral-genital sex relations.

Blow (one's) mind: to lose self-control or composure; to do something irrational, impolite; to be overwhelmed or deeply moved.

Blow out the afterglo: (1940's) to turn off electric lights.

Blow (one's) soul: (1950's) to do creative work with great passion and honesty.

Blow the gig: (1950's) to fail to appear for or at some (usually musical) job.

Blow the roof off: (1930's) to play loud music.

Blowtop: (prior to 1950's) an unstable or violent person.

Blow (one's) top: (1940's) to be completely overcome with enthusiasm, delight or pure emotion; insanity—like "flip one's lid," etc.

Blow up a breeze (storm): (1930's-40's) to play a musical instrument with great spirit and skill.

Blow your mind: to get high on a hallucinogenic drug or on an idea, or from seeing a good movie or painting or sunrise, etc.

Blow-your-mind roulette: a game wherein a variety of pills are thrown on a table or in the middle of a floor in a dark room and the players grope for and swallow the pills they find. Then they wait for their own reaction to see what they've chanced upon.

Blue: music sung or played in a "blues" manner; the sky or heaven.

Bluebird: policeman (obsolete).

Blue boy: according to Robert H. deCoy, in *The Nigger Bible*: "a Nigger male."

Blue Broadway: (1940's) the concept of heaven as it is associated with the sky; also, the Milky Way.

Blue funk: mental depression, extreme loss of will.

Blue note: in jazz, an off or flat note (in music); a moderately flattened 3rd or 7th note of the scale that cannot be demonstrated in written music.

Blues: (since 1895) Out of Negro work songs, hollers and spirituals, this special type of music became popular through the vocal style of W.C. Handy around 1912. As the blues moved in to the cities, many other forms of jazz, such as the "boogie-woogie" and "bebop," grew out of it.

Bluff cuffs with the solid sender: (1940's) trousers with large ballooning cuffs.

Board: (1940's) to eat; the expression was somehow deduced from the concept of a lodger who is supplied with regular meals.

Bogard (Bogart): (1950's-60's) to act in a forceful manner; black people growing up during the 50's identified easily with tough-guys like Humphrey Bogart.

Bogue: drug withdrawal sickness.

Bogus beef: (1940's) groundless complaint or chatter.

Bombed out: overcome or dominated by an excess of narcotics.

Bomber: a very thick reefer (marijuana).

Bombs: (1940's) word used to explain the effect of Kenny Clarke's drum accent after bebop become simply bop.

Bondage: (1940's) in debt.

Bone: (1900's-30's) trombone; male sex organ.

Bonfire: (1940's) a cigarette or its stub.

Boo: (1930's) corruption of "jabooby," marijuana, so called because it sometimes induced anxiety or fear in the user—what is meant by a "bad experience."

Boo-boo: a mistake.

Boogaloo: see *Black Boogaloo.*

Boogerboo: a deceptive person.

Boogie bear: (1940's) ugly person.

Boogie-Woogie: (1930's-40's) a fast-stepping blues in which the bass figure comes in double time—traditionally associated with Kansas City jazz; also, the type of dancing done to that music;

in some parts of the South, a case of syphilis. Some people believe Cou-Cou Davenport coined the phrase and that it refers to the devil, the "boogie," and all the troubles associated with him.

Boojy: bourgeois.

Book: (1920's) repertoire of a musical group.

Boo koos: a large quantity of anything.

Boolhipper: a black leather coat.

Boom boom: (1940's) a pistol or shotgun; a western movie.

Booster: an expert thief, especially in department stores.

Boot: (1930's-50's) to make exciting music; a black person; to explain.

Booted on: (1900's-40's) to be informed; hip.

Boot-snitch: (1940's) information.

Booty: a woman's body.

Bop: scat singing or playing of an instrument; see *Bebop.*

Bopper, bopster: one who is devoted to bop music.

Boss: (1950's) the very best of anything.

Boston: (1900's-30's) an accented base piano style.

B.O.T.: balance of (imprisonment) time.

Bottle up and go: (1940's) to leave.

Bottom: a rundown, disreputable area in a black community.

Bottom woman: in a pimp's stable of prostitutes, the favorite and the one he can most depend on.

Boulevard cowboy: (1940's) the style of "wild" taxicab driving that is common in Manhattan, New York, and on the South Side of Chicago.

Boulevard westerner: (1940's) a reckless taxicab driver.

Bounce: (1930's-40's) a lightweight; fast-tempo style of music.

Bouncy in (one's) deuce of benders: (1940's) Uncle Tom mannerisms.

Bow wow: (1940's) a gun.

Box: (1920's-40's) a piano; later, any stringed instrument; also vagina; house; apartment; room.

Boxed: (1940's) overcome by narcotics or liquor.

Box fire: (1940's) cigar or cigarette.

Boy: (1920's-40's) heroin, so called because of the sexual sensation it gives.

Bozo: (1940's) a man; a funny man.

Brace o' broads: (1940's) the human shoulders.

Brace of hookers: (1940's) human arms.

Brace of horned corns: (1940's) aching feet.

Brass wigs: (1940's) army officers (Southern Negro college use).

Bread: money.

Break: among jazzmen, to stop while playing without missing the beat.

Break (one's) balls: to overexert one's self at a task.

Breakdown, break-down: (1920's-40's) a very popular and exciting dance started by black people in the South, picked up by whites; the music to which it is done is fast, loud and jazzy; also, to explain something, "break it down."

Breaking luck: the first trick of the evening for a prostitute.

Break it down: (1930's) get excited while playing music; see *Breakdown*.

Break it up: (1930's) to earn great applause.

Break out with: to suddenly come forth with something.

Break up: (1940's) to explode with convulsive laughter; see *Crack up*.

Breeze up: (1930's-40's) the utmost.

Br'er Rabbit: One of the many stories about a rabbit. The rabbit had always been a central figure in the folktales of many African cultures. As slaves in "the land of the free," black folk continued to make up stories about trickster rabbits who were able to survive the threat or attack of far larger animals. It was a type of tale that said something meaningful to the black heart.

Bright: the color of a light-complexioned Negro; daylight.

Brightening: (1940's) early morning.

Bringdown, bring-down: (1940's-50's) anything depressing; a joy-killing person; see *Drag*.

Bring (someone) down: (1930's) to depress or sadden; help to sober a person.

Bring out: to introduce an uninformed person to the in-group's life style.

Broad: (1930's-50's) a girl, woman; originally, a plump shapely female; the shoulder.

Bronco Jim: an American Negro cowboy from Texas who was a skilled horsebreaker.

Bronco Sam: an American Negro cowboy bronco buster.

Broom: (1940's) cigar; to walk or run.

Broom to the slammer that fronts the drape crib: (1940's) to go to the clothes closet.

Brother: see *Blood brother* and *Blood*.

Brothers in black: (1940's) male Negroes (Southern Negro college use).

Brown Abe: (1930's) a penny.

Brownie arcade: (1940's) an amusement shooting-gallery characterized by one-cent slot-machines.

Brush: (1940's) short for "brush off"; mustache; to defeat or beat up.

Brushes: (1920's) in jazz, thin drumsticks that, when used on the drum's surface, create a soft, muted effect.

Bubber: James Miley, trumpeter, born 1903, died 1932.

Bubble dancing: (1940's) washing dishes.

Buck: Wilbur Clayton, trumpeter, born in Parsons, Kansas, 12-12-1911; played with Count Basie.

Bucket: (1940's) a car.

Bug: (1940's) to annoy or irritate.

Bugged on: (1940's-50's) extremely enthusiastic about something.

Bugle: (1940's) the human nose.

Bull: lesbian.

Bulldagger: variation on *Bull-dyke*.

Bull-dyke: an aggressive female homosexual.

Bull of the woods: (1940's) president or dean of a college (Southern Negro college use).

Bullskating: (1940's) to brag (Southern Negro college use).

Bull's wool: (1940's) stolen clothes.

Bump, bumpty-bump the bump: (1900's-30's) phrase voiced while doing a dance where people bump hips.

Bunch of fives: (1940's) the fists.

Bunk: William Geary Johnson, composer and instrumentalist; born 1879, died 1949.

Bunnyhug: (1900's-20's) jazz dance originating on the Barbary coast.

Burn: (1940's) to cook food or to cheat someone.

Burn for bread: to borrow or steal money; see *Burn*.

Businessman's bounce: (1930's-40's) monotonous dance music played with a society band.

Bust (one's) conk: (1930's-40's) to work very hard, especially mentally; see *Conk-buster*.

Busted: to be arrested or convicted.

Buster: William C. Bailey, clarinetist, born 7-9-1902 in Memphis, Tenn.; played with W. C. Handy's orchestra.

Bust (one's) nuts: to have an orgasm or to ejaculate.

Butch: female homosexual.

Butter-and-egg man: (1920's) a sarcastic phrase for vulgar, showy men who thought themselves bigshots.

Butterfly: (1940's) a good-looking young woman.

Butterhead: a Negro who is an "embarrassment" to his race.

Button (one's) lips: (1940's) to refrain from speaking.

Buzhies: black bourgeoisie.

Buzz: (1930's) the first effects of smoking marijuana or using some other kind of "dope"; telephone call.

Buzz mute: (1930's) an unusual instrument that creates a sound like a cross between a trumpet and a razor.

C

C: cocaine.

Cab: Cabell Calloway, singer and band leader, born 12-24-1907, in Rochester, N.Y.; famous "scat" singer of songs like "Minnie the Moocher."

Cack: (1940's) to fall out or to go to sleep.

Cakewalk: (1890's-1920's) a syncopated dance originating among Southern black people.

Calling the wind: see *Come wind.*

Call off all bets: (1940's) to die.

Camel walk: (1900's-40's) dance in which the emphasis is on imitating the shoulder and back movements of a camel in motion.

Campy: (1950's) cozy to the point of absurdity.

Canary: female jazz vocalist, especially one who sings with a band; one who informs against someone.

Candy man: (1960's) drug-pusher.

Cannibal: one who indulges in oral-genital sex.

Cannon: a pickpocket.

Cannonball: Julian Edwin Adderley, alto saxophonist, tenor trumpeter, born 9-15-1928 in Tampa, Fla.

Cap: glycerin container for drugs.

Capon: (1940's) an effeminate male.

Cap on: (1940's-50's) to censure; see *Dirty Dozens.*

Capped: (1940's-50's) to have outdone someone.

Carrying: possessing narcotics.

Carrying on: having an illicit affair.

Carve: (1920's-40's) to outplay another musician in a musical competition.

Cashmere: a sweater of any material.

Cat: (1920's-30's) originally, a jazzman; the female sex organs (an infrequent use); (1940's-50's) generally, anyone male.

Catch: (1920's-50's) to listen to or observe someone.

Catch up bass: (1900's) expression for the left-hand effect created by a jazz bassist.

Catfish trouble: (from a Louisiana folktale) a person's dog might have, instead of fleas, crabs; and by the same "logic" it is not improbable that a trouble-ridden person might one day catch in his mouse trap a catfish rather than a mouse.

Cathouse: a whorehouse; barrelhouse; a style of music.

Catting: (1920's-30's) when a man is out searching for available women; see *Tomcat.*

Cattle train: a Cadillac.

Cave: (1935) a room; pad; where one lives.

Century, to: to save up to a hundred dollars.

C & H: cocaine and heroin.

Chamber of Commerce: (1940's) a toilet.

Change: money, coins; in jazz, since about 1925, an interlude during which a "key" change is made.

Changes: on a personal basis, to have problems or to undergo a change of life style; in jazz, same as for *Change* except with more intense improvisation and innovation.

Changes, go through (put through): (since about 1952) to endure a series of intense emotional or psychological reactions; see *Changes.*

Changes, run the: (1947 and after) in jazz, to perform harmonic progressions as straight work, without genuine inspiration.

Channel: (since 1945) to cause two things to happen because of a particular initial move; a bridge, connecting separate entities.

Charge: (1935-) a thrill, especially from drugs.

Charles: white man; see *Charlie.*

Charleston: a dance step originated in the 1920's; done to a syncopated rhythm, it has been compared to a fast fox-trot.

Charley Goon: policeman.

Charlie: a corruption of "Mister Charlie," any white man; originally, the overseer or boss.

Charlie Nebs: policemen.

Chart: (1950 and after) in jazz, a written arrangement.

Chase (chorus): (1940's) jazz term—players in turn take a series of choruses each and go through a range of bars.

Cheat: (1910-25) in jazz, stretching harmonic or rhythmic variations to cover limited musical skill.

Cheaters: (1930's) dark eyeglasses; later, supplanted by *Shades.*

Check the war: (1940's) command to stop arguing (Southern Negro college use).

Check your nerves: (1940's) command to keep cool.

Cherokee Bill: a Negro cowboy, born in 1876 at Fort Concho Texas; a black cowboy, woman-charmer and infamous murderer who met his end on the gallows at age twenty.

Chewers: (1940's) teeth.

Chib (chiv): (1940's) an especially long and sharp switchblade knife.

Chick: a young woman, especially an attractive one.

Chicken feed: (1940's) an insufficient amount of money.

Chicken scratching: an ineffective beginning.

Chickenshit: very little and insufficient.

Chili: to ignore.

Chili pimp: one who plies his trade with only one prostitute.

Chill: (1940's) murder.

Chime: (1940's) time according to the clock.

Chimer: (1940's) any sort of time-piece but especially an alarm clock; the human heart.

Chimney: the human head; a hat.

Chinch: bedbugs.

Chinchpad: (1940's) a rundown rooming house or hotel.

Chinchy: (1930's-40's) stingy.

Chine: variant pronunciation of machine, automobile.

Chining: driving a car.

Chippy: one who infrequently uses strong drugs.

Chirp: (rare since about 1935) a female vocalist.

Chit'lins (Chitterlings): a traditional soul food—pork innards, considered waste by the slaveholder and therefore given to slaves who ritualized and turned it into a delicacy.

Chitt'lins 101: (1960's) derogatory phrase applied to any Black Studies course in U.S. schools.

Choice: (1947-52) excellent.

Choker: (1940's) a necktie.

Cholly: (1940's) a dollar bill.

Chop(s): (1925 and later) one's musical technique; lips or the mouth; a musician's lips.

Christian's path: Negro slave's term for a good, upstanding lifestyle.

Chubbyfat: extreme obtuseness.

Chu Berry: a tenor saxman, born in Wheeling, West Virginia, 9-13-1910 and died 10-31-1941; worked with Fletcher Henderson, among other outstanding artists.

Chuck: a white man; see *Charlie.*

Chump change: a small amount of money.

Chunk: to throw.

Circus love: an orgy.

Citizen: a square or prosaic white person.

Clam: (1950's) in jazz, a misplaced note.

Clambake: (1930's) a jazz or rhythm-and-blues musical affair that doesn't come off well.

Classis Chassis (Classy Chassis): an attractive young woman's body.

Claws: (1940's) fingers.

Clay-eater: a native of the lowlands of Georgia and South Carolina.

Clean: (since about 1925) originally, having no money; (1930's) being free of drug addiction; also, in musical terms, technically precise; (1950's-60's) free from suspicion, generally.

Clean out of sight: unusually impressive.

Clink: a Negro.

Clinker: (since the 1930's) in jazz, an error in playing; at one time also referred to the leg chain that bound one convict to another in a chain gang.

Clip: (1940's) to steal something, especially to pick someone's pocket.

Clip side of big moist: (1940's) on the other side of the Atlantic Ocean where the war (World War II) was going on.

Clock (clocker): (1940's) the heart.

Clockwork: (1940's) one's mind.

Cloud (followed by a number): expresses contentment, the kind of ease associated with the floating light-weightedness of clouds; *example*, Cloud 7 or Cloud 9.

Clown: (1940 and after) a foolish person, a "typical" down-home nigger; see *Nigger*.

Cluck: (1940's) black or very dark; a very black Negro.

Clyde: an uninformed person, a square.

C and M: cocaine and morphine.

Coast: the feeling of being "high" or "stoned," utter relaxation as a result of using drugs.

Cock: a black girl's sexuality or organs. Interesting, this reference is *male* by orientation and is used that way by whites but in provincial black communities it has a *female* meaning—the influence of the matriarchy?

Cocksman: a male whore.

Cocktail: to stick the last bit of marijuana ("roach") into the cleaned-out end of a regular cigarette because it is too short to hold by hand. Also, the "roach" may be wrapped into the torn-off flap of a book of matches to achieve the same end.

Coffee-bag: (1940's) a pocket.

Coins: money.

Coke: cocaine.

Coke-frame: (1940's) shapely female body compared to the contours of a Coca-Cola bottle.

Coke-head: cocaine addict.

Cold: a *mean* action, incident or experience.

Cold in hand: without money.

Cold meat party: (1940's) a funeral.

Collar a broom: (1940's) to leave.

Collar a duster up the ladder: (1940's) to climb steps.

Collar a hot: (1940's) to eat lunch or supper, especially very fast.

Collar the jive: (1930's-40's) to grasp what is happening in a situation.

Colly: to comprehend, to understand.

Colt: (1940's) young man.

Combo: (1930's-40's) abbreviation for "combination," a small musical group as opposed to a big band.

Come again: (1940's) a request to repeat or restate what has been said.

Come down: (1930's-40's) to start sobering up from the body-and-mind effects of drugs, including liquor.

Come off: (1930's-40's) to return to normal from the effects of a drug stimulant; to stop.

Come on: (1930's) a person's manner of acting or approaching people or situations.

Come on like Gang Busters: (1940's) do something in a very fast and stunning way.

Come on strong: (1950's) positive behavior (complimentary).

Come out: to be introduced to the "happenings" in the hip world.

Come wind: a cry that was customary among black people during slavery when a task was dependent on wind currents.

Comp: (1940's) in jazz, a shortening of "accompany."

Compy: (1940's) variation on the word comprehend.

Con: (1920's-40's) to trick, persuade or promote in someone's mind an idea he or she may not have previously entertained.

Confession: (1940's) a conference with a teacher (Southern Negro college use)—take-off on the Catholic Confession.

Conjuring lodge: stemming from their belief in the power of the conjuror, black Americans during slavery held this as a place in which mediumistic practices could be respected and practiced.

Conk: (1940's) pomade for the hair; the human head itself.

Conk-buster: (rare since 1940's) generally, anything that proved mentally difficult; also sometimes referred to what drugs or liquor did to the mind.

Conkpiece: (1940's) the head.

Connection: one who sells drugs; a person who can obtain dope; contact man for narcotics.

Conniggeration: apparently invented by Robert H. DeCoy for his book *The Nigger Bible*. He says it means, in essence, the love of black people for each other—the process of demonstrating affection and interest in the interrelations between what he calls "Nigrites."

Cook: (1930's and after) in jazz, to play with great inspiration; to be in the spirit of a situation; also, a method of dissolving heroin with water in a spoon over a flame.

Cooker: (rare since 1950's) a hip or swinging person.

Cookie (ey, ee): the female genitalia.

Cook up: to cook heroin.

Cook with gas: (1940's) to be really informed and in the spirit of any popular fad.

Cool: (1940's and after) loosely used, but generally means anything favorably regarded; a word of agreement; also, a cool person is one who is detached, aloof.

Cooling: (1935) in jazz context, not employed.

Cool it: to take it easy, go slow.

Cool jazz: (since 1948) a style of jazz associated with musical developments on the West Coast, usually mellow and restrained, sometimes referred to as intellectual music.

Cool out: calm down or to restrain an urge toward enthusiasm.

Cool papa: (1940's) a nonchalant male.

Cooning: *stealing* as opposed to robbing. This word may have been picked up from white usage.

Coonjun (Coongiv): to be exploited (Southern Negro use).

Cooper: black roustabout working the hogsheads at the Louisville tobacco auctions at the end of the 19th century. There were many of them.

Cootie Crawl: (1916-20) a popular jazz dance.

Coo-yon: one who is crazy (perhaps regional, New Orleans).

Cop: to obtain something, especially drugs.

Cop a broom: (1940's) to leave in a hurry.

Cop a drill: (1940's) to leave at a walking pace.

Cop a nod: (1940's and after) to take a nap, to sleep.

Cop a plea: (1935-55) to be verbally evasive.

Cop a squat: (1940's) to sit down.

Cop out: (1950 and after) to make excuses for one's self; evasiveness; to rely on an alibi.

Copper-nose: (1940's) a drunk.

Copping Z's: sleeping.

Corn: (1940's) money.

Corn bread: a soul food, sometimes referred to as hoecakes or fritters; also, hot-water corn bread. Made from cornmeal. Other variations stemming from corn bread: corn-bread dressing; molasses corn cakes; corn dumplings, frequently served with turnip greens.

Cornfield hollers: a loose phrase for Negro work songs.

Corn pone: personality with the flavor of a Southeasterner.

Cotton: the hair of a woman's pudendum.

Count Basie: born William Basie, 1904, in Red Neck, New Jersey; world-famous band leader, composer, pianist; winner of many jazz polls and mentor of an impressive number of now-famous singers and instrumentalists.

Cow Cow Davenport: born Charles Davenport at Anniston, Ala., 1894; died in Cleveland, Ohio, 1955; as pianist and singer he toured (1914-30) the vaudeville circuit; author of the famous *Cow-Cow Boogie.*

Cow express: (1940's) shoe leather.

Cow pea soup: soul-food vegetable often cooked with ham bones and onions.

Cozy Cole: born William Cole in East Orange, New Jersey, 1909; drummer; first recordings were done with the famous Jelly Roll Morton in 1930; later worked with Louis Armstrong and Benny Goodman.

Crab: (1940's) a college freshman (Southern Negro college use).

Cracked-ice: (1940's) diamonds.

Cracker: a white person. One theory holds that it's a term from the 19th century back-country of Georgia, coined by black people —a reference deriving from the whip-*cracking* slaveholder. Another theory is that it comes from the white soda cracker as opposed to, say, ginger cookies.

Crackling biscuits (bread): oven-cooked bread containing dried pork skin, a soul food.

Crack up: (1950's) convulsive with laughter.

Crack wise: an obvious square who uses a profusion of hip terms in an effort to be accepted on the "scene."

Crazy: any thing, person or place that is beautiful; the *n*th!, great or good.

Crazy rim: a handsome hat.

Creaker: (1940's) an old person.

Creep: a clandestine mission usually referring to a romantic meeting between male and female.

Crib: (1940's) one's home or room, rare after coinage of *Pad*.

Croak: to die.

Cross: short for "double-cross"; to deceive or mislead or confuse.

Cruising: looking for or making contact for sex relations.

Crumbcrusher (snatcher): (1930's and after) a baby or small child.

Crumb-hall: (1940's) a dining room.

Crumbs: (1950's) an insubstantial amount of money.

Crumb-stash: (1940's) a kitchen.

Cruncher: (1940's) a small child who eats a lot; the sidewalk.

Crutch: a car.

Cubby (hole): a room or a *small* apartment where one lives.

Cue: a tip, money given to a waitress or waiter as a token of gratitude.

Cuffee: (African word) black person.

Cupcake: (1940's) a pretty girl.

Cups: sleep, asleep.

Cut: (1920's) in jazz, to outdo a competitor in playing a solo; (1930's) the tapes done during a recording session; (1960's) any musical work or theatrical performance.

Cut a rug: to dance, especially to jitterbug.

Cut a swath: anything impressive. Stems from early field-hand use to characterize any great amount of work done with a scythe.

Cute suit with the loop droop: (1940's) a flashy, drape-like suit of clothes.

Cut loose: to make a break with a situation or person.

Cut no ice: the failure to convince or win or impress someone.

Cut out: (1940's) to depart or leave.

Cut rate: (1940's) to belittle someone.

Cutting (carving) contest: (1930's-40's) in jazz, a "battle" between musicians wherein the applause of the listeners serves as a grading system.

Cutware bottoms up: (1940's) the act of holding a drinking glass upside down to the mouth in order to drain it of its last liquid drops.

D

Dabbling: moderate use of narcotics.

Dad: (rare since 1940's) word of address by one male to another.

Dada Mama: (1920's) a drum roll.

Daddy: (1920's-40's) usually a woman's term of address to her male lover.

Daddy-O: term of address by one male to another, demonstrating affection, respect and sympathy.

Daddy week: (1940's) Daddy was nickname for Frank Schiffman, managing director of Harlem's Apollo Theater, and "week" refers to the usual span of time bands and acts were employed.

Dagger-pointed goldies: (1940's) a yellow, sharp-toed style of shoes.

Damper: a savings bank or safe-deposit box.

Dance in the sand box: to jive, to scheme.

Dap: (1950's) dapper, dressed in style.

Date: (1920's) recording appointment (for musicians); also came to mean (1950's) a *Gig*.

Davy Crockett: (1940's) draft-board official.

Day gig: (1940's) also known as a *Slave*— a non-musical job a musician is forced to take for need of money.

Deadbeat: one who does someone out of something.

Deadly: excellent.

Dead president: (1940's) any paper certificate of money.

Dead thing: (1960's) a phrase used to refer to any white idea or manner or custom or artifact.

Deadwood Dick: believed to have been a Negro cowboy, Nat Love, a slave born in Tennessee (1854-55?). He left home at 15 to work with a cattle outfit. The men of Deadwood City (Dakota Territory), because he won a very popular shooting contest, bestowed upon him the name "Deadwood Dick." In the 1870's many adventure stories about Deadwood Dick began to appear and were read mostly by boys, but Nat Love in 1907 published a book about his real adventures.

Deb: girl member of a gang.

Decked out: the particular way one is dressed.

Deece: (1940's) a dime.

Deep hole: problem situation.

Deep sin: (1940's) a grave.

Deep sugar: (1940's) a romantic statement usually by a male to a female.

Defense plant on square's dim: (1940's) Amateur Night at Apollo Theater in Harlem.

Dem: *deliberate* corruption of "them"; refers to white people.

Demon: (1940's) dime.

Den: (1940's) one's home.

Derby: the reference is to the human head as it relates to oral copulation.

Desk piano: (1940's) a typewriter.

Deuce: (1920's) two dollars or a two-dollar bill; a pair.

Deuce o' dims and darks on the cutback: (1940's) forty-eight hours ago.

Deuce of benders: (1940's) knees.

Deuce of demons: (1940's) two dimes.

Deuce of haircuts: (1940's) two weeks.

Deuce of nods on the backbeat: (1940's) two nights ago.

Deuce of peekers: (1940's) two eyes.

Deuce of ruffs (russ): (1940's) twenty cents.

Deuce of ticks: (1940's) two minutes.

Dey: white people; see *Dem.*

Dick: (1940's) a term of address among beboppers; later replaced by Jack or Jim.

Dicty (Dickty, Dictee): a high-class or snobbish-acting person or a way of acting haughty.

Dig: (1930's and after) to understand; a call for attention (like "Hey!") or an expression of understanding, like "I dig."

Dig the dip on the four and two: (1940's) to take a bath every Saturday night.

Dig you later: (1930's and after) an expression of farewell; it was shortened to "later."

Dim: refers to nighttime or evening.

Dime: ten-year prison term.

Dime note: (1935) ten dollars.

Dime's worth: ten-dollar bag of marijuana or morphine.

Dims and brights: (1940's) days and nights.

Dinky: poor quality.

Dip: a hat.

Dipping: picking pockets.

Dip, The (Beale Street): (1912-16) jazz dance in vogue.

Dirt: gossip; an objectionable person; (1920-35) earthy jazz usually played by small bands.

Dirty: (1920's and after) bad or mean, terrible.

Dirty bird: nickname for Old Crow Whisky.

Dirty dog: any man who mistreats a woman (definitely a woman's expression).

Dirty Dozens: a very elaborate game traditionally played by black boys, in which the participants insult each other's relatives, especially their mothers. The object of the game is to test emotional strength. The first person to give in to anger is the loser. See *Signify.*

District, The: (1910-17) the section of New Orleans known as Storyville, famous as a place where early jazz went through its "urban" birthpains.

Dittybop: a young person who crudely and foolishly displays hip mannerisms that are out of key with his or her personality.

Dixie (land): name of the first or one of the first famous jazz bands to appear in New Orleans restaurants around 1917; a *style* of music characterized by the combined tonal effects of a sax, a trumpet, a clarinet; pre-Swing music.

Diz (Dizzy): John Birks Gillespie, born in Cheraw, S.C., 10-21-1917; trumpet-player, composer, singer, jazz-band leader; a very famous jazz personality and musician who (in 1951) started his own recording company.

Do: short for hairdo.

Doc Cheatham: Adolphus Anthony Cheatham; trumpet player; born in Nashville, Tenn., 6-13-1905; worked with Cab Calloway, Herbie Mann and Billie Holiday.

Dog: an old whore; an unfair man; and, rarely, an exceptional person.

Doghouse: (early 1940's) bass violin or string bass.

Dog's howl: a warning of coming disaster, especially if it occurs at night.

Dog tune: (1940's) a jazz song of poor quality.

Doing a hundred: in very fine shape.

Doing the dirt: a moral judgment implying something bad.

Do it: (1920's-30's) a phrase often cried out in encouragement to one who was already demonstrating any sort of cultural refinement or artistic skill.

Dome: (1940) the human head.

Domie (Domi, Dommy): (1930's) one's home or apartment.

Don't make bah-nahn: one lover to another: "do not disappoint me." (Possibly limited to New Orleans).

Don't sweat it: don't worry, take it easy.

Doodle: (1900-35) in jazz, to play with great informality.

Doo-hicky: generalized name for any object (usually a mechanical device); sometimes one whose name has been momentarily forgotten.

Door sign: any object (such as a horseshoe) placed above a doorway out of respect for the particular beliefs and fears of the people within; a very old custom going back to and beyond the ancient Jews who considered the doorway (as symbol of the "doorway of life") sacred and best protected by "magic."

Dope: information; at times also used to refer to illegal drugs but mainly in mockery of "square" usage.

Dots: (1920's) in jazz, first referred to musical notes on sheet music and later to the sheet music itself.

Do up: (1940's and after) to cause something to happen; to effect change; tie a cord around the arm to distend vein for injection of heroine.

Down: (1940's) word of approval citing excellence, especially in a person's character, particularly when he exhibits an earthy, unpretentious personality; (1960's) *down* was replaced by *Together.*

Down home: (1950's) an honest, unpretentious life style or personality; in jazz, an earthy way of playing.

Down on: harboring bad feelings against someone.

Down with: (1930's and after) to be in command of something; to understand a subject completely.

Down with (one's) ax: (around 1955) in jazz, to be skilled in the professional use of an instrument; proficiency in working with one's materials.

Dozens, The: see *Dirty Dozens.*

Dozzing (Dossing): sleeping or napping, especially as a result of the effects of drugs.

Drag: (1900) a musician who lags behind the beat "drags" it; a blues style, a tempo; (1940's) a bore, a dull person, place or incident; also feminine attire when worn by a homosexual, especially to a social affair.

Drape(s): (1930's) a keenly draped zoot suit; to be "draped" was to be attired in the best of Harlem fashion.

Dream box: the human head.

Dribble: (1940's) to stutter.

Dried-barkers: (1940's) furs.

Drilling: (1940's) walking.

Drink: (1940's) any large body of water like an ocean or river.

Drop: an orphan, especially one whose parents are unknown.

Drumsticks: (1940's) human legs.

Dry goods: clothing.

Dry long so: ((1940's) dullness or fate.

Ducks: (1940's) tickets to any social event.

Dud Bascomb: Wilbur Odell Bascomb, trumpet player, born in Birmingham, Ala., 2-16-1926; played with Erskine Hawkins.

Duds: (1940's) clothes.

Dues: (1940's and after) the ups and downs of life; one's responsibilities or commitments.

Duke: Edward Kennedy Ellington, composer, pianist, band leader, born in Washington, D.C., 4-29-1899; in himself, a living institution of modern American culture; famous as the composer of such classics as "Sophisticated Lady," "Solitude," "In a Sentimental Mood," and "I Got It Bad and That Ain't Good."

Dukes: (1940's) especially the fists but also refers to knees.

Dumplings: flour, salt, corn meal mixed with water, often cooked with turnip greens—soul food.

Dunk sauce: left-over cooking liquid.

Dust: (1940's) to leave; money.

Dust-bin: (1940's) a grave.

Dusted: killed or buried, usually as an act of revenge.

Duster: (1925-45) the buttocks; see *Rusty Dusty.*

Dusty butt: (1900-45) an ineffective, ugly prostitute; also a short person whose rear end, as the term implies metaphorically, drags along on the ground.

Dynamite (dyno): undiluted drugs.

E

Early beam: (1940's) in the morning.

Early black: (1940's) in the evening.

Early bright: (1930's) the first daylight of the morning; dawn.

Early candlelight: a way of measuring evening time before watches and clocks became common household objects.

Ear man: (1917-40's) a musician who does not read sheet music, who plays rather "by ear."

Ear music: (1917-40's) improvisational music.

Ears: (1940's and after) to listen; *example,* "I got *ears* for what you're saying"; sometimes implies approval of what is being heard.

Earth pads: (1940's) feet or shoes.

Eat it up: to enjoy (anything) immensely.

Eel-ya-dah: (1940's-50's) black existential verbal jazz sounds originating in bebop.

Eight ball: a "square" person; an unsophisticated person.

Eight-to-the-bar: (1930's-40's) the Boogie-woogie, a dance.

Eighty-eight (88): (1940's) a piano.

Elizabeth Club: an all-female social club where Negro domestic workers get together informally.

Enamel: (1940's) human skin.

End, the: (1950's) of the highest order; superlative.

-Est: (1950's) superlative; the *n*th degree.

Every tub (on its own black bottom): (1920's-40's) in jazz, improvisation independent of any prearrangement.

50

Evil: (1930's) usually a reference to a particular person or an "unnatural" *effect*, meaning bad or very terrible.

Evil eye: refers to the superstitious belief that the eye(s) of a person can generate "evil" enough to "jinx" or even to kill, as, "if looks could kill." Probably stems from the notion that the eye reveals true human emotions; although especially believed by black American slaves, this superstition recurs in many cultures.

Expense: (1940's) a newborn baby.

Explosion: (1940's) in jazz, a very loud burst of chords.

Eyeball: to look, to see.

Eyes: (1940's and after) an expression of approval or desire, as in, "I got eyes for her"; "big eyes" mean possessing great desire or approval, "no eyes" expresses aversion or disapproval.

F

Face: (1940's) a stranger, especially an unknown white person.

Fade: a Negro who fades into a white way of life.

Faded Boogie: a black informer; a white nigger.

Faggot: a male homosexual (derogatory).

Fake: (1915-45) in music, to make the best of a lean situation; to sing or play without other musical backing.

Fake book: (1920's-30's) a record book of chord progressions used by jazz musicians working at dances.

Faker: (1915-45) a musician with no command of written music.

Fall apart: (1940's) to experience extreme excitement.

Fall by (in, up): (1940's) act of arriving.

Falling star: believed by many (black and white) to represent the spirit of someone who has made a pact with the devil.

Fall off (drop off): (1920's) in jazz, to lower the instrumental tone by playing or blowing which reduces the volume.

Fall out: (1930's) to be surprised or overcome.

False (fake) fingers: (1920's) in jazz, a way of "choking" the trumpet with the fingers to produce certain desired effects.

Family jewels: testicles (term used by homosexuals).

Fan: to flaunt one's self.

Fangs: (1950's) a musician's lips and teeth and fingers; also, his skill; see *Chops.*

Far out: something that defies any convention or established mode.

Fat: (1930's and after) in jazz, a full tone; also wealthy.

Fat cat: an impressive, wealthy person.

Fat city: a fine state of affairs.

Fat lip: obnoxious talk.

Fats: jazzman.

Faust: (1930-45) a blind date, an ugly girl.

Feature: (1935-45) an expression of enthusiastic approval.

Feed: (1940's) in jazz, chords backing a soloist.

Feel a draft: the sensing of racism in a white person, especially when directed against oneself.

Feelers: (1940's) fingers.

Feeling: (1930's-40's) emotional honesty; see *Soul.*

Feel (one's) stuff: (1930's-40's) to operate out of one's deepest and truest feelings.

Fell: (1940's) to be put in prison or to endure any terrible condition.

Fews and twos: (1940's) a small sum of money.

Few tickers: (1940's) a few minutes.

Fiddle-cases: (1940's) shoes.

Field nigger: originally a black slave who worked crops, as opposed to one who worked in the home of the slaveholder. Malcolm X extended and popularized the concepts: a field nigger was more likely to become a revolutionary while the house nigger was more likely to be an Uncle Tom.

Fifty-eleven (Fifty-'leven): a profusive or uncountable quantity.

Fillmill: (1940's) a tavern.

Filly: (1940's) a young woman.

Final thrill: (1940's) death.

Fine and mellow: (1930's-50's) very satisfying.

Fine as wine: (1930's-50's) quite pleasing.

Fine fryer: (1940's) an attractive young woman.

Finger(s): a jazz pianist; sometimes also means pickpocket.

Finger artist: a lesbian.

Finger-popping: excited snapping of fingers in time to jazz; a very spirited listener is said to be finger-popping (probably originally used more by white jazzmen than black).

Fire: (1940's) cigarette.

Firsts: traditionally, Negroes who are the first of their race to occupy a given position of prestige in any American career.

First thirty (30): (1940's) the month, January (a common phrase despite the fact that January has 31 days).

Fish: a woman.

Fish-hooks: (1940's) fingers.

Fish horn: a saxophone.

Fives, the: (1920-35) a piano blues style; funky; (1940's) fingers.

Fix: usually, an injection of heroin; a bribe.

Fixing: preparing for an occasion.

Fizzical culturist: (1940's) a bartender.

Flag spot: (1940's) bus stop.

Flagwaver, flagwaving: (1930's) the high point in a jazz performance.

Flappers: (1940's) arms.

Flaps: (1940's) ears.

Flat: (1940's) a nickel; an apartment; without money.

Flat-backer: heterosexual prostitute.

Flick, flicker: (1940's and after) a motion picture; the theater itself.

Flip: originally to overwhelm; (1950's) either enthusiastic response or violent response; to lose one's head.

Flip (one's) lid (top): (1940's-50's) to go crazy; to be insane.

Flippers: (1940's) ears.

Flipping out: (1960's) temporary psychotic reaction to drugs.

Flip side: (1940's) the opposite side of a wax record of recorded music.

Floating: intoxicated on one kind of drug or another.

Fluff: (1930's) especially in jazz, to play a false note; to goof; to get rid of someone or something; to snub.

Fly: (1900's-40's) to be fast and ecstatic; brash.

Flychick: (1940's) a pleasure-loving, party-going young woman.

Flyer with the roof slightly higher: (1940's) a modified version of a ten gallon Stetson hat.

Focus: (1940's) to look.

Fold (one's) ears: to advise, especially at great length; also simply to talk impressively to someone.

Foreign: refers to what are considered unnatural sex acts.

Forget it: implies that the listener has not properly understood what is in question or being explained; *example,* "if you think this dictionary was easy to put together, *forget it!*"

Forks: (1940's) fingers.

Four and one: a workman's payday; Friday.

Fox: (1940's-60's) a beautiful black girl.

Fox trot: (1917) a phrase that attempted to define a type of jazz dance and rhythm.

Foxy: female beauty, especially black.

Frail: (1940's) a thin girl.

Frail eel: any good-looking woman.

Frame: (1940's) the body; a suit of clothes.

Frantic: (1940's) anything exciting and satisfying.

Freak: (1920's) one who practices socially unaccepted forms of sexual love; (1940's-50's) a strong believer in something.

Freak lips: (1920's) in jazz, a musician who possesses the skill to play high notes (brass) for an impressive length of time; see *Iron lips.*

Freebee(s): (1900-60's) things or ideas that do not cost money.

Freeze on: to ignore a person or situation.

Fresh water trout: (1940's) good-looking girls.

Frisking the whiskers: (1940's) the "warm up" playing musicians do before swinging into a full jam session.

Frolic pad: (1940's) a nightclub or dance hall.

From (out) front: (1940's-50's) from the very beginning.

From hunger: (1930's) of inferior quality.

Front: (1940's) a suit of clothes, particularly an expensive one; (1950's-60's) false appearance.

Fruit: (1930's-40's) to "jive" around; (1950's) a homosexual.

Fruiting: (1940's) being promiscuous.

Fry: to straighten (with a hot comb) nappy hair.

Fucked up: (1940's-70's) confused or experiencing great misfortune, or both.

Funk: (1950's) the "soul" quality in black music, the melancholy mood of the blues; also known as *South, Hard bop* and *Down home.*

Funky: (1950's) a "nittygritty," truly felt blues mood in jazz and therefore in the people who produce this art form; sometimes called "a sense of tragedy" in Euro-American logic.

Funky Broadway: the main street where the underbelly in any city shows.

Funny: strange.

Funny-looking: odd.

Fuss: crying (Southern use).

Fuzz: (1930's-40's) police.

G

Gabriel: a trumpet player, especially professional.

Gage (Gauge): (1930's) marijuana.

Galloping piano: (1920's-30's) in jazz, a rhythm that sounds much like a hoof gallop.

Gal officers: (1940's) harpies, lesbians.

Gam: to brag, show off.

Gam cases: (1940's) stockings.

Gander: (1940's) to walk.

Gang: (1930's-50's) a large amount of anything; see *Boo Koos*.

Gang-shags: lively parties, real jam sessions.

Gangster: marijuana, especially a rolled joint.

Gaper: (1940's) a mirror.

Gas: (1940's) anything enormously surprising, exciting and satisfying; (1950's) word was stretched (losing its character) to mean anything very unusual, amusing.

Gas buggy: (1930's) automobile.

Gas meter: (1940's) a quarter.

Gasper: (1940's) a cigarette.

Gas pipe: (1940's) a trombone.

Gasser: (1930's-40's) anything excellent.

Gat: a firearm (maybe derived from "Gatling Gun").

Gate: (1920's-40's) jazz musician or any hip male person (coined by Louis Armstrong).

Gatemouth: gossiper.

Gator: (1920's) short for Alligator; one male friend to another.

Gay: homosexual (male).

Gazer: (1930's-40's) a window.

G.B.: goof ball.

Gee: (1930's-40's) male friend or any male.

Geets: (1940's) power or money or both.

George: any Negro Pullman porter (picked up from white usage).

Georgia cracker: a white person of that state.

Georgiaed: to be misused in any way, similar to what happens in *the Murphy.*

Georgia skin: a card game similar to Gin Rummy.

Get around: (1930's-40's) to overcome a difficulty.

Get go (gitgo): the beginning.

Get hot: (1920's-40's-50's) in jazz, to play with great excitement; in gambling, to have a "streak" of luck.

Get in there: (1930's-40's) command to become active toward a positive end.

Get it: (1920's-50's) a cry of encouragement to one engaged in doing something positive and exciting.

Get (one's) jollies: to have fun, experience pleasure.

Get (one's) kicks: see *Get (one's) jollies.*

Get (one's) nuts off: sexual release, implies ejaculation more than orgasm.

Get off: to experience the relief of injected drugs, especially after a taxing hassle to come by the stuff; in jazz, musical improvisation; as a sexual reference, ejaculation or orgasm.

Get-out: a person's clothing.

Get previous: to act in a very forward manner.

Get (one's) rug beat: (1940's) to get a haircut.

Get some kick: (1940's) to obtain money.

Get to: effect.

Get (one's thing) together: mainly, to orient one's thinking and living to whatever the popular political and social notions happen to be.

Get up: to get high; or to refrain from something.

Get with it: to be physically and psychically in fashion or in the spirit of what is happening, usually a command.

Ghost note: (1920's) a soft, almost unheard jazz note in a series of louder ones.

Gig: originally a jazzman's job; later it came to mean any kind of job.

Gig around: working at any number of jobs.

Gims: (1940's) the eyes.

Gin: a street fight or melée.

Gin mill: a run-down nightclub, especially where a jazz musician finds himself working, grudgingly. Musicians who have experienced drugs have contempt for the sloppiness of heavy drinkers or any drinking crowd.

Girl: cocaine, so called because of the sex-like feeling it gives; also, a male homosexual.

Gitbox: (1920's-40's) guitar.

Give a shit: to care.

Give (one) five: two people slapping their hands together, a motion of agreement.

Give out: (1930's-40's) an outpouring of feeling or talk.

Give (one) some slack: to show restraint; a plea for more sympathy and understanding.

Give (one) some sugar: to kiss.

Give the drummer some: handslap acknowledgment; see *Give (one) five.*

Glad pads: (1940's) dance halls or other lively places.

Glimming: the act of seeing.

Globetrotter: an addict who moves fast and frequently.

Glory: the Negro slave's term for the Christian concept, Heaven.

Glory roll: (1930's-40's) a large roll of money carried in the pocket, especially to impress others with.

Glue-sniffing: inhaling fumes of model airplane glue in order to get stoned.

Go: (1920's) an enthusiastic expression of encouragement, especially to a jazz performer making music.

Goat hair: bootleg liquor.

Gobble: (1920's-40's) to talk.

Go-down: (1940's) a basement apartment.

Gofer: one who "goes for" something; an expression of approval.

Go for soul: an all-out expression of deeply felt excitement.

Go home (let's): (1920's-40's) an agreement among jazzmen to do the final chorus of a number.

Going high: a long-lasting intoxication.

Golden leaf: (1920's-40's) very good marijuana.

Gold fish: (1940's) sliced peaches.

Go-long: a truck used by policemen to transport large numbers of arrested people to jail; a paddy wagon.

Go-man-go: (1940's) a cry of encouragement, especially to a performer of one kind or another; see *Go*.

Gone: (1940's-50's) anything unusually exciting and good, sometimes to the extent of being unreal; in a trance; crazy.

Gonest: (1940's-50's) the best.

Goo: (1920's-50's) sticky food or human blood.

Good hair: straight or almost straight hair (a concept that began to disappear in the early 1960's with the renewal of black consciousness).

Good stick: nausea and vomiting after use of heroin; considered not unpleasant.

Goof: (1940's-50's) a mistake, to make a mistake; a stupid person.

Goo-goo watch: (1930's-40's) the early hours of morning.

Goola: (1900's-40's) piano.

Goon squad: (1960's) mediocre political leadership; cops.

Gorilla: the act of strong-arming someone.

Gorilla pimp: a stupid, crude, tactless hustler.

Gospel: the Negro slave's expression for The Truth.

Gospel plow: the Negro slave's term for The Righteous Way of living.

Got (one's) boots on: (1940's) to be wise, hip.

Go to town: any activity accompanied by extreme excitement.

Go-up: (1920's-50's) an upstairs apartment.

Go-up Salt River: (1940's) to die.

Government-inspected meat: a soldier or sailor (homosexual term).

Grabbers: the hands.

Grape-cat: (1940's) male who drinks a great deal of wine.

Grape-chick: (1940's) female who drinks a great deal of wine.

Grapes of wrath: (1940's) wine.

Grass: (1930's-70's) marijuana; also white folks' hair; see *Silk.*

Gravy: (1940's) money or the power it generates.

Gray, grey: (1930's-50's) white person.

Grease: to eat.

Grease (one's) chops: (1930's-60's) to eat.

Greasy fingers: a pickpocket.

Greasy junkie: indolent drug user.

Greasy spoon: a restaurant serving boiled and oily and fried foods, specifically associated with black culture; soul-food restaurant.

Great white father: (1930's-40's) usually the President of the United States but actually any extremely powerful authoritarian figure who happens to be white.

Green (Long green): (1950's) money; sometimes, a considerable sum of money.

Greyhound: to run fast.

Grit: (1940's) food.

Grizzly Bear: (1910-20) a jazz dance.

Groovy: (1930's-70's) excellent, enjoyable.

Ground apple: (1940's) a brick or rock or stone.

Groundgrabbers: (1930's-40's) shoes.

Groundpad spade: (1940's) a shoe horn.

Ground rations: sexual intercourse.

Growl: (1920's-40's) in jazz, a crude tone produced on the trumpet, thought of as lowdown and dirty.

Gully-low: (1900's-50's) in jazz, much the same meaning as *Growl;* in general use it refers to a poverty-ridden, unsophisticated life style.

Gum-beating: talking.

Gun: (1930's-40's) to look.

Gungeon (Jamaican ganga): potent marijuana, either from Africa or Jamaica.

Gunpowder: gin.

Gutbucket: (1900's-50's) a lowdown, "nittygritty" blues style of jazz originally played in *Gin mills*. (The word referred to the smaller bucket that served beneath the larger liquor barrels to catch the gin leakage in such places.)

Guts: (1930's-50's) emotional and spiritual honesty coming from the very bottom of the self; earthiness; see *Soul.*

Gutter (music): (1900's-30's) a type of Negro music originating in New Orleans; lowdown, "nittygritty" music.

Gutty: (1930's-40's) of the gutter; see *Gutter (music)* and *Guts.*

H

H: (1930's) heroin.

Habit: (1930's-60's) drug habit, usually refers to the heavy use of heroin.

Hack: anger or annoyance; a white person; a prison guard.

Hacked: (1940's-50's) irritated, exhausted.

Haint: may be defined as ghost, spirit, specter, phantom, apparition, a disembodied spirit (probably a corruption of *haunt*).

Haircut: to be robbed or cheated; to be abused in some way by a woman.

Half a stretch away: (1940's) the distance of one half of a city block.

Halfers: (1890-1900's) Southern Negro sharecroppers.

Half past a colored man: (1940's) 12:30 a.m.

Hall: (1900's-40's) any place where jazz musicians gather to perform.

Ham-bone soup: made with onions, celery, carrots, potatoes, tomatoes, green peas, turnips, and butter beans, plus one or more ham-bones—soul food.

Ham fat: (1900's-30's) mediocre person or thing.

Ham kick: (1900's) a social game designed to give men a peek at the underpants and thighs of girls; the girl who could kick a ham that was hung high up won the meat.

Hammer: beautiful Afro-American girl.

Hammer-man: an authoritarian figure.

Hams: (1930's-40's) human legs.

Handcuffs: (1930's-40's) an engagement ring or wedding ring.

Handkerchief head: an Uncle Tom; (1940's) one who wears a rag on his head to preserve his expensively processed hair-do.

Handsome ransom: (1930's) a large quantity of money.

Hang: a job, especially one taken or held grudgingly.

Hangout: a place for illicit sexual relations; meeting place for a gang.

Hangup: a problem, a psychological block.

Happenings, haps: (1940's-50's) usually refers to any significant incident or situation of the moment.

Happy: Albert Caldwell, tenor sax, born in Chicago, 7-25-1903; played with Bernie Young's Creole Jazz Band (1922).

Hard: (1930's-40's) like the word "bad," for black people "hard" has a positive connotation, *terribly* good.

Hard bop: (1950's) a blues-type bop, closer to an earlier form—hot jazz—than to straight bop; see *Funky*.

Hard-hitting: (1940's) timely, in style, anything excellent.

Hard John: (1940's-50's) an FBI agent.

Hardleg: any man or an ugly woman.

Hard-oil: (1940's) lard or oleomargerine.

Hard skull-fry: (1940's-50's) a heavily greased and shiny conked hair-do.

Hard spiel: (1940's) jive talk.

Hard swing: a very intense form of swing music.

Harlem-toothpick: (1930's-40's) a switch-blade knife carried in the pocket.

Harpie: (1940's) an old woman with an ulterior romantic motive.

Hash: short for hashish.

Hassle: to fight or argue; worry.

Hat: (1940's) any female; wife, sweetheart.

Haul ass: to run; go.

Have a thing about: an obsession with a person or an idea, but not necessarily negative like *Hangup*.

Have it covered: (1950's) to be completely in command.

Hawk: Coleman Hawkins, tenor saxophonist, born 1904; (1930's-

60's) the crisp, cold blast of winter winds that sweep city streets, as in Chicago from Lake Michigan.

Hawkins: (1940's) cold winter winds.

Hawk riding: (1940's) refers to music made by Coleman Hawkins.

Hay-eater: any white person.

Hay now: (1940's-50's) a greeting, like hello.

Head: (1920's) in jazz, any improvised musical arrangement well known by the players; (1930's) drug user; (1930's-60's) fellatio; bathroom.

Headbone: the human skull.

Headcheese: various cheap grades of pork meat prepared and sold as lunch meat.

Head-chick: (1940's) a man's favorite woman; a woman skilled in oral love-making.

Head hen: (1940's) a landlady or female manager of a rooming house.

Head Knock: (1930's-40's) God, the Lord, or Jesus.

Headlight(s): a light-complexioned Afro-American girl; any woman's breasts; diamonds.

Headquarters: a person with an unusually large skullbone.

Hear: (1930's) to *experience* jazz with "understanding."

Heat: law-enforcement officer.

Heavy: (1930's-70's) anything eminent and profound.

Heavy heat stretch: (1940's) the months of summer.

Heavy lard: (1940's) a very impressive verbally rendered story.

Heavy lump: (1940's) the section known as Sugar Hill, in Harlem.

Heavy soul: (1950's, rare) heroin.

Heavy wet: (1940's) a rain storm.

Hell: excellent; good; an impressive person.

Hen: (1920's-40's) usually any woman over thirty.

Hide: drums.

Hideaways: (1940's) one's pockets.

Hide-beater: (1930's-40's) drummer.

High: (1900's-50's) intoxicated.

High hat: (1930's) jazz, a foot-pedal-operated double cymbal.

High-powered: (1940's) excellent, stylish, timely; see *Hard-hitting*.

High yaller (yella): light-skinned Afro-American, especially female.

Hike: (1940's) to hide a valuable object.

Hinges: (1930's-40's) one's elbows.

Hinges creaking: (1930's-40's) old age.

Hinkty: (1930's-40's) a snobbish or pompous person.

Hip: (1950's) sophisticated, independent and wise; in fashion; alert and courageous. Became popular again in the 1960's and 70's.

Hippie (hippy): (1940's) a person who tries without success to be hip; over-blasé; a would-be hipcat. In the 1960's the word fell largely into white use and took on a more specific meaning, referring to the generation that followed the youngest of the "Beat Generation" of New York and San Francisco.

Hipster: (1940's) a hip person, knowledgeable.

Hit: to take a puff on a reefer; a quantity of anything.

Hit (one): to refill one's whisky glass; to win; to say "hit me" while playing cards, for example, is to ask for a card from the deck.

Hit on: (1940's-50's) to make a request, especially for love-making.

Hit the road, Jack: a command to someone to leave.

Hobo cocktail: (1940's) a glass of water (Southern Negro college students' use).

Hocks: (1940's) the feet.

Hog maw: pig's stomach.

Holding: (1940's) possession of illegal drugs.

Holy roller: a fire-and-brimstone preacher or church member.

Home: (rare) a term of address used by two black people either from the same Southern state or simply from the South (Southern use).

Homeboy: person from one's home town (Southern).

Home-cooking: (1940's) anything fine, not especially food.

Homey: (1930's-40's) a newly arrived Southerner in a Northern city.

Honey, a: (1940's) a beautiful thing or person.

Honkey: a white person; (Southern use, originally); an ice-cream bar.

Honking brown: (1940's) a flashy tan suit of clothes.

Honkytonk: (1900's-20's) in jazz, a "low" style of life; see *Gutbucket, Barrelhouse.*

Hooch: liquor.

Hoochy-choochy (man or woman): one who practices voodoo.

Hooked: (1930's-40's) addicted.

Hooks: the human hands.

Hoop: (1940's) a ring.

Hop: (1930's-40's) to dance.

Hop a twig: (1940's) to die.

Hoppergrass: grasshopper.

Horn: any reed or brass wind instrument.

Horse: (1930's-50's) heroin.

Horse blanket: (1940's) an overcoat.

Horse heavy: (1940's) fat person.

Hotbed: (1930's-40's) in a flophouse a public bed for the price of 25 cents per eight hours.

Hot dog!: a cry of excitement.

Hot jazz: (1920's-40's) a loud, unpolished style of music, usually with a very heavy beat, far removed from "popular" or "commercial" music.

Hot shot: a poisonous injection of heroin.

Hound: to pester, annoy; Greyhound bus.

House band: (1900's) a jazz orchestra engaged on a permanent basis in one location.

House of countless drops: (1940's) a barroom in which grilled food as well as liquor is sold.

House of D: Women's House of Detention on Greenwich Avenue, N.Y.C.

House of knowledge: (1940's) a school, especially a college.

House of pain: (1940's) a dentist's office.

House without chairs: (1940's) an apartment or flat where dancing is permitted.

Hubba hubba: (1940's) an expression of approval.

Humbug: anything perplexing or complicated or both.

Hummer: (1940's-50's) a small error; also getting something free.

Hump: (1930's-50's) a difficulty; the more physical aspects of sexual intercourse.

Hung, Hung-up: (1940's-70's) inhibited; confused; paranoid.

Hurting: to be in extreme need or misfortune.

Hustle: (1900's-60's) to survive by any means possible; self-employment on a makeshift job.

Hustler: (1900's-60's) see *Hustle.*

Hype: deception; an addict; phoney situation; scheme.

I

Iced: imprisoned and in solitary confinement.

Ice-palace: (1940's) a jewelry store.

Icky: (1930's-40's) sentimental, tasteless.

Idea-pot: (1940's) the human skull; one's mind.

Igg: (1930's-40's) ignore; shun.

In-and-out-of: (1940's) any doorway.

Index: (1930's) the human face.

In front of: to have control of a situation; to possess the solution to a problem.

Ingest: (1950's) a suffix used as though it were a word in itself, meaning the greatest, the *n*th.

Ink: cheap wine.

Inky-dinky: (loosely used) a negative connotation, sometimes refers to a very dark Afro-American who happens also to be untidy.

Insane: (1940's) positive, healthy state of mind.

Insiders: (1940's) one's pockets.

In there: (1930's-40's) sophistication; hip; informed.

Into something: (1950's) creative, special, involved, intelligent, lucky, unusual or exciting.

Iron lips: see *Chops* and *Freak Lips.*

Irregardless: irrespective.

Israelite: (1940's) any Jewish person (mainly Harlem use).

Issue: (1940's) any situation or thing or person.

Ivories: (1900's-40's) piano keys.

Ivory tickler: (1900's-40's) a pianist.

J

Jack, Jackson: (1930's-40's) term of address by one male to another.

Jackie Robinson: any black person who is the first to penetrate a social or professional category.

Jam: (1930's-50's) to make exciting music; to have a good time socially; to "party."

James Brown, the: a dance originated by James Brown, singer.

Jams: real and imaginary prisons.

Jam session: (1930's-40's) an occasion where jazz musicians get together to play strictly for their own pleasure.

Jasper: lesbian.

Jazz, jass: (a French word meaning sexy or sensuous) attempts to define various kinds of musical forms created and developed primarily by black Americans—from the African *beat*, spirituals and work songs, to the music of the New Orleans marching bands, the Story-ville district, the barrelhouse and cathouse musical innovations; also high spirited.

Jazzy: (1930's-40's) old-fashioned; brash; (1950's-60's) in style; up-to-date.

Jeff: (1930's) a white person; to inform on someone; a dull person; a horrible square.

Jelly: (1930's-40's) without charge.

Jellybean: (1930's-50's) a term of address.

Jelly-roll: (1890's-1900's) one's lover, spouse; (1920's-40's) a term for the vagina.

Jelly-Roll Morton: Ferdinand Joseph La Menthe, composer, pianist, band leader, singer, born in Gulfport, La., 9-20-1885, died in Los Angeles, Calif., 7-10-1941; a great figure in jazz history.

Jersey highball: (1940's) cow's milk.

Jersey side of snatch play: (1940's) to be over forty.

Jesse James Killer: (1940's) any heavy, gluey hair pomade with a sharp scent.

Jessie: (1940's) a red-head "vixen."

Jib: mouth.

Jick head: a drunk.

Jiffy: in a hurry.

Jim: (1940's) term of address to a male; see *Jack.*

Jim Crow: enforced segregation. (Term comes from the song *Jim Crow,* featured in a Negro minstrel show by Thomas Rice 1808-1860.)

Jitterbug: (1930's-40's) a dance done to swing music; the Lindy Hop.

Jitterdoll: (1940's) a woman who loves dancing.

Jitterjane: (1940's) any woman who dances a lot and enjoys it.

Jive: (1920's-30's) to sneer; (1940's-50's) deceit; to put someone on (may be a distortion of the English word "jibe"). Often intensified by the suffix "ass," as in "jive-ass."

Jodie: the *Dictionary of American Slang* explains the word this way: "A civilian male; one who has been rejected by or deferred from the draft . . ." but the real meaning has come to be that Jodie is back home making love to the enlisted man's wife.

Joe blow: (1920's-40's) originally any horn-blowing musician but came to mean any male person.

Joe Sad: one without friends, unpopular.

John: any man; when used by a prostitute means same as *Trick,* but especially a white male.

John Henry: a hard-working black man; a black man with courage and endurance in the face of inhuman work.

Joint: (1930's-40's) where one lives; the penis; (1940's-70's) marijuana wrapped in cigarette paper.

Jones: a fixation; a drug habit; compulsive attachment.

Journey: the Negro slave's term for life on earth.

Joy box: radio.

Joy juice: (1940's) liquor.

Jug: (1900's-30's) bottle containing liquor.

Jug band: (1900's-30's) usually a small musical group in which a bottle or jug is used as a music-making instrument.

Juice: (1930's-40's) liquor.

Juice back: to drink liquor.

Juiced: (1930's) drunk.

Juicehead: (1930's) a person who is frequently drunk.

Juice joint: (1930's) tavern, bar, cabaret.

Juke (jook): (1900's-30's) a whorehouse, roadside-inn life style; the type of music played in a "juke joint." The music itself is characterized by an excessive use of stringed instruments.

Juke box: public coin-operated record playing machine.

Jump: (1930's) any lively dance done to swing music; music with a bouncing rhythm.

Jump in: (1930's-40's) to become involved.

Jump salty: (1930's-40's) to suddenly become angry.

Junebug: nickname for one who is named after his father.

Junk: (1930's) narcotics.

Junkie: (1930's-40's) drug addict.

Juvey: reform school.

K

Kack: (obscure) used much in the same way as "fellow" or "dude."

Kapow! Kapow!: vocal sound made in imitation of a gun being shot (probably picked up from comic strips).

Keep on keeping on: perseverance.

Keep the faith, baby!: (1960's) a slogan made popular by the Congressman from Harlem, Adam Clayton Powell, during his self-exile and much-publicized expulsion from Congress. It was addressed to black people and means: remain optimistic, despite everything, regarding the goal of self-determination.

Keister: buttocks.

Kelt, keltch: white person; Negro passing for white.

Kemels: (1940's) shoes.

Keyholding a round tripper: (1940's) to be witness to an extraordinary event, such as a home-run at a baseball game or love-making through a keyhole.

Kick: (1930's) thrill; to overcome a drug habit; (1940's) one's passion or activity; satisfaction; a fad.

Kicks: one's pleasure; shoes; also, that which is laughable.

Kill: (1930's-40's) to affect strongly; *example,* "You kill me!"

Killer-diller: (1930's-40's) inscrutable but exciting.

Killjoy: (1940's) a policeman or any official person.

Killout: a fascinating person or an extremely exciting situation or thing.

Kiss-off: (1940's) to die.

Kite: a note delivered in prison; air mail letter.

Kitty: Cadillac, also known as *Hog.*

Kitty, kitten: (1930's) very young and inexperienced person, especially a girl.

Klook: Kenny Clarke (also known as Liaquat Ali Salaam), drummer, born in Pittsburgh, Pa., 1-9-1914; important jazz musician.

Knobs: (1940's) one's knees.

Knock: to criticize negatively; (rare) to borrow or loan; to speak or walk.

Knock a nod: (1940's) to go to sleep.

Knocking her dead one on the nose each and every double trey: (1940's) to get a paycheck every sixth day.

Knocking off hen tracks on a roll top piano: (1940's) to type a personal letter on a typewriter.

Knock off: to take, to do, to stop.

Knockout, knock out: (1930's-40's) much the same as *Killer-diller;* some thing or person not easy to understand but nevertheless considered very excellent and thrilling.

Knock up: to impregnate.

Knotholes: (1940's) doughnuts.

Knowledge box: the head.

Knuckle with (one): to fight physically.

Kong: home-made whisky.

Konk: the human head; grease.

Kopasetic: (1940's) excellent.

L

Lace curtains: the prepuce (homosexual term).

Lady, Lady Day: (1940's) Billie Holiday, 1915-1959, great blues singer.

Lamb: (1940's) an innocent person who is easily deceived.

Lame: (1950's) an unsophisticated act or person; wrong.

Lamp: (1920's-40's) the act of seeing.

Lamps: (1920's-40's) one's eyes.

Land of Darkness: (1930's-40's) the Negro section in any town or city.

Larceny: an unkind or evil feeling or open condemnation of another person.

Large: (1930's-40's) successful, thrilling, well-to-do.

Large charge: (1930's-50's) great excitement.

Last debt: (1940's) death.

Last heart-beat: (1940's) one's sweetheart.

Last out: (1940's) death.

Latch for the gate to your front yard: (1930's) one's collar pin.

Latch on: (1930's-40's) to understand or take part in an activity; to become aware.

Later: (1950's) a manner of saying goodbye, short for "see you later"; also, a put-down; *example,* "Later for that jive, man!"

Law: (1900's-20's) the police.

Lay across the drink: (1940's) the continent of Europe.

Lay back: (1930's) in jazz, to lag behind the main rhythm; in everyday life, to go slow, unhassled.

Lay dead: to wait; do nothing; also, to hide.

Lay down: (1930's-50's) to explain; to outline a theory; to present.

Lay (some) iron: (1900's) to tap dance.

Lay on: to give.

Lay (bread) on: to lend or give money.

Lay (something) on (someone): (1930's-50's) to relay a message; to give.

Lay out: to avoid.

Lay up: (1930's-50's) the same as *Lay dead*, but especially in one's own home.

Lazy: (1900's) to be calm, relaxed.

Leadbelly: Huddie Ledbetter, singer, guitarist, born at Mooringsport, La., in 1888; died in New York City, 12-6-1949; world famous as a folk singer.

Lead sheet: (1940's) one's top or overcoat.

Least: mediocre or dull person or situation.

Left town: (1900's) to have died.

Legit: in jazz, a "straight" or conservative musician.

Leg sacks: (1940's) socks.

Lemon: light-skinned Afro-American or mulatto.

Let (one) down for (one's) chimer: (1940's) to steal someone's watch.

Let it all hang out: (1960's-70's) to be uninhibited, free.

Let it lay: (1940's) command to forget something.

Let the good times roll: (1900's-20's) a cry for enjoyment—music, talk, drinking, etc.

Let up: command to restrain from verbally abusing someone.

Liberty: (1940's) a quarter.

Lick: (1930's-40's) a plan, an idea, outline of a situation.

Lickety-split: the sound of fast motion, any kind, or of working fast.

Lickety-splup: (1900's) a hard-luck song, sung by Negro crap-shooters in Georgia. It goes: "Lickety-splup, lickety-splup/ the more you put down, the less you pick up." (*American Negro Folksongs,* by Newman I. White, Folklore Associates.)

Licking the chops: (1940's) the tuning up musicians do before a jam session.

Licks: (1920's-40's) very jazzy musical notes.

Licorice stick: (1930's-40's) clarinet.

Lid: (1930's) the sky; one's mind; a hat or cap.

Light bread: white bread.

Light drips: (1940's) a Spring shower.

Lighten up: a plea for compassion or restraint.

Lightly and politely: (1930's-40's) to effect smoothly, as though without effort.

Lightning bugs: (1940's) cigarette tips burning in a dark room.

Light splash: (1940's) a bath.

Like: (1940's-70's) a word that bridges gaps in spoken sentences; *example*, "Like, man, I was out in Wyoming, like two years and it was like, wow!"

Like cheese: (1940's) any strong odor.

Like it is (telling it): the real condition as one sees it.

Like Jack the bear (just ain't nowhere): (1930's-40's) an expression of disappointment, worthlessness, wounded ego, etc.

Lily-white: a reference to U.S. white Anglo-Saxon Protestants; white person who is always conscious of being white; bed sheets.

Limp wrist: having latent homosexual tendencies.

Lindy (hop): (1927) a popular dance first done at the Savoy; named after Charles A. Lindbergh.

Line: the purchase price of an item; (1940's) smooth talk, usually directed by male to female.

Lines: money.

Line the flue: (1940's) to eat.

Lip: a defense lawyer; talking back in self-defense.

Lip-splitter: jazzman who in blowing his horn is frantic; inflammatory; a deadly fighter.

Lipton's: (1940's) fake or poor marijuana.

Little Eva: a loud-mouth white girl.

Little Jazz: Roy Eldridge, trumpeter, singer, drummer, born in

Pittsburgh, Pa., 1-30-1911; famous as a trumpeter and prolific recording artist.

Little mama: a black girl, usually attractive.

Living room gig: in jazz, a T.V. appearance.

Loaded: possessing a great amount of something; very "high" or "stoned."

Lobo: (1940's) an ugly girl.

Lobstertails: (1940's-50's) usually refers to a case of crabs; sometimes, a venereal disease.

Lock up: (1940's) to possess completely.

Long bread: (1940's) a great deal of money.

Longhair: (1930's-40's) musicians who play from written music; the kind of commercial music they play; a deep subject or an intellectual.

Loot: (1930's-40's) money; cash.

Love letter: (1940's) a bullet or rock thrown at someone.

Low down: (1900's-40's) the blues; an economically depressed life style: see *Gutbucket, Barrelhouse, Blues*; also, the inside information.

Lugs: (1940's) one's ears.

Lumpy: in jazz, playing that sounds that way.

Lung-dusters: (1940's) cigarettes.

Lush: (1930's-40's) a person who drinks a great deal.

Lush hound: (1940's-50's) a drunk.

Lushie: (1940's) a drunk.

Lying: (1950's) to play music without sincere emotion.

Lynch: to kill (a person) by any means.

M

M: (1930's) morphine.

Ma: a prefix often added to a male homosexual's name by his intimate friends.

Macking: pimping.

Mad: (1940's) used loosely, this has a positive connotation: great, exciting.

Made: had one's hair straightened (female).

Mah-shu-ka-tin: gossip (New Orleans).

Main Drag of Many Tears: (1940's) 125th Street, Harlem. So called because of its many poverty-stricken and disappointed people who try to laugh away their tears.

Main kick: (1940's) stage in a theater.

Main man: a favorite male friend; one's hero.

Main on the hitch: (1940's) a woman's favorite man, especially her husband.

Main queen: (1940's) a man's wife or favorite girl-friend.

Make: to do.

Make change: work or do something to obtain money.

Make it: to go; to cope; to take part in sexual love-making; to perform; to succeed at something.

Make like: to imitate.

Make (one's) love come down: orgasm; to make love; to be aroused passionately.

Make the scene: (1950's) to go to the place, usually a street corner where one's friends gather, or a pool room, barbershop, or some other public place; also, one "makes the scene," especially if one is dressed distinctively. (Two novels dealing with the subject: *The Scene,* by Clarence L. Cooper, Jr., and *Corner Boy,* by Herbert A. Simmons.)

Make tracks: to leave; to run; to go away in a hurry.

Making it: to barely subsist; to succeed; to leave a place.

Mama: a pretty black girl.

Man: a word brought into popular use by black males to counteract the degrading effects of being addressed by whites as "boy"; black males address each other as one man to another.

Man in gray: (1940's) the letter-carrier from the post office.

Mantanblack: (1960's) physically very black.

Man, the: policeman, and white authority-figure; one's white boss.

Man who rides the screaming gasser: (1940's) policeman in a patrol car.

Man with headache stick: policeman.

Man with the book of many years: (1940's) judge in a courtroom.

Map: (1930's-40's) the face.

Maps: sheet music.

Marble town: (1940's) a cemetery.

Mark: an innocent man who can be used; a trick; a sucker.

Mary Ann: marijuana.

Mary Jane: (1950's) marijuana.

Mashed Potatoes: a dance originated by James Brown; see *The James Brown.*

Mason line: (1940's) the main street, especially one indicating the boundary between a black and a white community. An obvious take-off on the actual Mason-Dixon line that serves as a marker between the North and the South.

Mass action: (1940's) refers to communism.

Mat: one's wife or sweetheart.

Mater Mazuma: (1940's) a female college teacher (Southern Negro college student use).

Mean: (1900's) the finest; good; down-to-earth; honest; strong; (1900-1940's) possessing soul; gutbucket spirit; funky.

Me and you: short for, "It's going to be me and you"—a way of saying, we're going to fight.

Meet: a jazz gathering; gig; jam session.

Mellow: (1930's-40's) gentle, sincere, satisfying; cool.

Mellow-back: fashionably dressed.

Melted out: (1940's) to be without money and desperate.

Member: (1950's) one black person to another: club member, member of the race.

Mess: (1900's) large quantity; also, to say to someone, "You're a mess," is to imply that he or she is remarkable or puzzling.

Message: (1950's) the sensation felt from music well communicated; to understand something that is not clearly or not at all stated.

Mess around: (1920's-30's) popular improvisational jazz dancing.

Messed up: troubled; confused; victim of bad luck.

Messy: (1930's-40's) unusual.

Meter: (1940's) twenty-five cent coin.

Mezz, Mezz's roll: (1940's) a generous and potent stick of marijuana, the kind rolled by Mezz Mezzrow, well-known jazz personality, a white man who for many years lived in Harlem; author of *Really The Blues.*

Mice: (1900's-30's) violins.

Mickey Mouse (music): popular, commercialized music, put down by jazzmen; weak, background music.

Miff: Irving Milfred Mole, trombonist, born in Roosevelt, L.I., 3-11-1898; best known for his Dixieland music.

Mighty Dome: (1940's) House of Congress or any government building.

Mighty Mezz: see *Mezz.*

Mikes: (1940's) the ears.

Mind in the mud: (1940's) vulgar thoughts.

Miss Ann: a white woman—carry-over from Southern terminology, but now used with a good-natured sneer or with outright maliciousness.

Mister B: William Clarence Eckstein, singer, born in Pittsburgh, Pa., 7-8-1914; became a very famous nightclub soloist.

Mister Charlie: a white man—carry-over from Southern use, with no friendly over- or under-tones; see *Charlie*.

Mister Hawkins: a cold winter's wind; see *Hawk*.

Mister Speaker: (1940's) a pistol, especially a revolver.

Mister Tom: a middle-class Negro; see *Tom, Uncle Tom*.

Mitt man: a religious imposter who capitalizes on the devoutly religious people who are his victims.

Mitt pounding: (1940's) applause.

Mitts: (1940's) hands.

Moldy: out of style.

Moldy fig: (1940's) one who rejects the new jazz in favor of forms innovated during the 1920's and 30's.

Monkey: (1920's-40's) a band or orchestra leader.

Moo: money.

Mooch: (1920's-30's) a slow dance similar to the *Drag;* (1940's-50's) to beg or borrow.

Moo juice: (1940's) cow's milk.

Mootah (mooter, muta, mu): (1930's) marijuana.

Mop: (1940's) the last beat at the end of a jazz number with a cadence of triplets; one's natural hair.

Mose: (1940's) a Negro.

Moss: (1940's) one's hair.

Most: (1950's) the best.

Mother: an effeminate male; homosexual; drug-pusher. Some variations: mutheree, motherferyer, motherfouler, motherhugger, motherjiver, motherlover, mothersuperior, mammyjammer, mammysucker, mammyfucker, mammyhugger.

Motherfucker: any male; the connotation is not necessarily negative.

Motorcycle: a woman. The implication is that one can "ride" either.

Motorcycle bull: (1940's) traffic law enforcement officer.

Mouse: (1940's) one's pocket.

Move: (1950's) impressive, exciting.

Moving out: (1950's) demonstrating great imagination and originality; being dynamic.

Mow the lawn: (1940's) to comb the hair.

Mucty-muck: meaningless talk or lies.

Mug: (1940's) the human face.

Mugged behind five: (1940's) speaking with the hand shielding the lips.

Mugging: (1930's-40's) making funny faces; making love.

Mugging heavy (or light, lightly): (1930's-40's) in jazz, the term refers to the beat, its quality.

Muggle: a cigarette with marijuana stuffed into its tip; see *Roach.*

Mulligrubs: the blues.

Murder: (1930's-40's) excellent; the best.

Murphy: a con game played on innocent men (especially white) who are expecting sex with a prostitute (usually black). The pimp or hustler steers the *Trick* toward a vacant place where he waits for a woman who does not appear. The pimp has, of course, already collected the "bread" (money) and "split" (gone).

Muscle: bluff; false.

Mush: (1940's) a kiss.

Mutt: Thomas Carey, trumpeter, born in New Orleans, La., 1892; died in Los Angeles, Calif., 9-3-48; played with King Oliver in Dreamland.

My man: (1930's) an especially friendly term of address by one male to another.

N

Nab: policeman.

Naked jazz: gutbucket; low-down.

Name: (1930's) well-known person.

Napoleon: (1940's) an insane man.

Nappyblack: (1960's) very African-looking.

Naps: kinky hair.

Nasties: sexual desire.

Nasty: (1900's-40's) sexy; down-to-earth; good; terrible; mean.

Natch: (1940's-50's) variant of "naturally."

Nat King Cole: Nathaniel Coles, singer, pianist, born in Montgomery, Ala., 3-17-1917; became a very popular vocalist, his first big hit "Straighten Up and Fly Right."

Natural: (1930's) an intensifier used with many other words such as "a natural born freak"; (1960's) a look, among American black people, inspired largely by positive racial identification with emerging "free" Africans who are bringing their countries onto the stage of the technological world.

Neck-breaking it: to move swiftly.

Negro: (1960's-70's) to call someone a Negro is another way of calling that person an *Uncle Tom;* see *Uncle Tom.* The word Negro, in itself, does not qualify as a slang term except in this sense of renaming something. The acceptability (or the lack of acceptability) of terms black people use for self-identification have been always in a state of flux. A new generation traditionally rejects the terminology of the preceding one.

New thing: (1960's) in jazz, an aggressive and original attitude and feeling, as demonstrated in the music of artists like Ornette Coleman, Eric Dolphy, Cecil Taylor, John Coltrane, Sun Ra, Pharoah Sanders, et al; in black writing, the "new thing" trend is best indicated through the works of writers who appear in the anthology *The New Black Poetry.*

Nice: to feel very well in all or any respects; *example,* "I'm nice."

Nickel note: (1940's) five-dollar bill.

Nigger: (possibly from the French *negre* when used by a white person in addressing a black person usually it is offensive and disparaging; used by black people among themselves, it is a racial term with undertones of warmth and good will—reflecting, aside from the irony, a tragicomic sensibility that is aware of black history.

Nigger-lover: a white person who associates with or who relates to black people on a human level—a white term, originally offensive and disparaging.

Nitty-gritty: unvarnished facts; underbelly of a situation; core; the basics.

Nix out: (1940's) to throw away.

Nod: (1930's-60's) stupor-like state experienced by a junkie succumbing to drugs, usually in a standing position.

Noggin: the head.

Noisola: (1930's-40's) a record-player.

Noodle: (1930's) in jazz, to play in a testy manner; also, the human head.

Nookie: vagina; sexual intercourse.

Noose is hanging: (1950's) a state of readiness.

Nose wide open: to have one's "nose wide open" is to be in love.

No stuff: an expression that implies sincerity.

No sweat: easy to manage.

Nothing happening: (1940's-50's) often a response to "What's happening?" The implication is that things are more than simply slow.

Nowhere: applied to a really dull or square person who is also undesirable; also, a place or thing of the same quality.

Number one: a person's best-loved sweetheart or spouse.
Nut: orgasm; testicles.
Nut roll: one who plays stupid.
Nutty: (1950's) superior.

O

O: (1930's) opium.

O-bop-she-bam: an existential jazz phrase; perhaps a mystic effort to comment on the inscrutable in the black man's social, moral, and spiritual condition in the United States, or simply another way of talking *to* that "sense" of mystery often referred to as God.

Ofay: white man (foe in Pig Latin).

Ofay watcher: an oppressed person who carefully observes whites and their actions (see *Soul On Ice,* by Eldridge Cleaver).

Offbeat: (1900's-40's) in jazz, prior to 1935, a cymbal note hit by the drummer; odd; fantastic.

Offed: murdered.

Office piano: (1940's) a typewriter.

Off the cob: (1940's) out of style or backwards.

Off-time jive: (1930's-40's) a weak excuse.

Oil: graft, pay-off to authorities.

Oiler: (1930's-40's) one who is prone to fist-fights.

Oink: (1960's) a cop; policeman; law-enforcement officer.

O.K.: "orally korrect," a phrase Andrew Jackson used to initial paper work as a symbol of his approval; it is *an American* term used widely by Afro-Americans.

Okey-doke: white values, ideas; a "con game" or stupid talk.

Oldie: (1900's-20's) an old song or tune.

Old lady: (1900's) one's mistress; (1920's-50's) one's wife.

Old man: (1900's) one's male lover; (1920's-50's) one's husband.

Old man Mose: (1940's) death or time.

Old massa (marster): Negro slave term of address to a white slave-holder, variant pronunciation of *old master.*

Old saw: (1940's) one's wife.

On: (1940's-50's) informed, sophisticated; "in."

One bill: a hundred dollars.

One-night stand, one-nighter: (1920's-50's) a booking for one appearance in a nightclub or theater.

On ice: in prison, in solitary confinement.

Onion act: (1940's) anything or situation considered extremely wrong.

On the beam: (1940's) smart, alert.

Oo-bla-dee: see *O-bop-she-bam.*

Oofus: (1930's) a dumb, awkward person.

Oowee: (1940's) an expression of shock or delight or excitement.

O.P.B.: (other people's brand) reference to a hypothetical brand of cigarettes.

Orchestration: (1940's) an overcoat.

Other man: (1930's-40's) the white man, especially one who is a merchant in a black neighborhood.

Out: (1940's-50's) a show of great imagination and skill; *example,* "His music is way out!" Also, extremely unusual.

Outfit: the various artifacts used by an addict; see *Works.*

Out of it: (1950's) unfashionable; unpopular idea, etc.

Out-of-sight: (1950's) extremely exciting or revolutionary (idea or person or thing).

Out of this world: (1920's-40's) same as *Out of sight.*

Out to lunch: (1960's) to be off; to miss the point; to be confused; neurotic; vague.

Over: (1950's) to get "over" is to accomplish an objective.

Oxford: (1940's) a Negro whose complexion is very dark (from *Oxford* shoe polish).

O.Z.: (1930's) an ounce of marijuana.

P

Pad: (1930's) one's home; room; apartment.

Paddles: (1930's-40's) the hands.

Paddy: a white person.

Pad of galloping snap-shots: (1940's) motion picture theater.

Pad of stiffs: (1940's) a funeral parlor (Southern Negro college student use).

Pad of stitches: (1940's) a hospital (Southern Negro college student use).

Pail: (1940's) the stomach.

Pale: a white person.

Pan: (1940's) one's face.

Panatella, panatela: (1930's) the finest grade of marijuana.

Pancake: an Uncle Tom or servile person.

Panicky: (1940's) extreme pleasure or excitement.

Pants: (1940's) any male person.

Papa: Oscar Celestin, cornetist, band leader, born in Napoleon-ville, La., 1-1-1884; died in New Orleans, La., 12-15-1954; played with Henry Allen, Sir's Excelsior Brass Band.

Paper: (1900's-40's) sheet music.

Paper doll: (1940's) to play hookey from school; to leave.

Paper man: (1900's-40's) a musician, especially a drummer, who plays according to written music.

Paradiddle: (1900's) a very basic drum roll.

Party piano: (1920's-40's) a sort of fast-moving style, like Lil Hardin's; boogie-woogie; a blues pattern as theme.

Paws: (1940's) the hands.

89

Pay dues: to have hard luck; to suffer as a result of race prejudice; to have come up the hard way.

Payoff: (1940's) a person who is free with his or her money.

Peck: short for *Peckerwood*; a white person; also, to eat.

Peckerwood: originally, any very poor Southern white Anglo-Saxon Protestant. The word came into use as a result of the vivid presence in the South of the red woodpecking birds that black people saw as a symbol of whites; on the other hand, they saw the common black bird as a symbol of themselves. The word was turned around to preserve the privacy of its meaning and origin. Later, it took on a more general meaning—any white person—and especially during the 1950's it was used widely even in many Northern black communities.

Peck horn: (1900's-20's) mellophone or saxophone.

Pecking: (1950's) in jazz, a fast, abbreviated style like Charlie Parker's or, before him, Art Tatum's; (1930's-40's) a jitterbug dance step originated at the famous Cotton Club in the late 30's.

Peckings: (1940's) food.

Peekers: (1940's) the eyes.

Peeling a fine green banana: (1940's) making love to a very pretty light-skinned girl.

Peep: (1940's) in jazz, to read sheet music; also, simply *to see*, especially with great understanding.

Pee wee: (1900's-50's) small; a very narrowly rolled marijuana cigarette.

Peg: (1930's) trousers tapered down to the cuffs.

Peola: (rare) a light-skinned Afro-American girl.

People: narcotic agents; sometimes also refers to one person; *example*, "He's good people."

Pez: (1940's) mustache, goatee, beard or the hair on one's head.

Phiz: (1940's) the face.

P.I.: (1900's) pimp.

Piano: spare ribs.

Piano kid: (1900's) an early jazz term: any pianist working the run-down joints.

Pic, piccolo: (1930's-40's) juke box.

Pick cherries: (1900's) playing bass or guitar.

Pickers: (1930's-40's) the fingers.

Pick up (on): (1930's-50's) to listen, to observe; to take, to obtain.

Pick-up band: (1930's) a quickly brought together assortment of musicians for the purpose of a recording or concert.

Picnic: to have fun; a pleasant experience.

Piece: (1900's) a pistol; musical instrument; female sexuality; an ounce of heroin, referred to as "piece of stuff."

Pies: (1940's) the eyes.

Pig: (1960's) a policeman.

Pigeon: (1920's-40's) a young woman; a person who informs on another.

Pigeon dropping: (1940's) confidence game-playing.

Pig meat: an older, loose woman; a dumb girl; female whore.

Pile of bricks: (1940's) any building in a city.

Pillars: (1930's) human legs.

Pillow pigeons: (1940's) bedbugs.

Pimp steak: (1940's) a frankfurter.

Pinchers: (1940's) shoes.

Pine drape: (1940's) a coffin.

Pinetop: Clarence Smith, 1904-29; well-known vaudeville singer, pianist and songwriter.

Pink: (1900's-40's) white person.

Pink chasers: (1900's-40's) black people who deliberately cultivate friendships with white people.

Pink pimp suit: crib.

Pinktoes: a black man's white girl friend; a white girl.

Pinky: (1940's) Afro-American girl who looks white; term popularized by the movie *Pinky*, starring Jeanne Crain.

Pinning: to look or gaze.

Pins: (1940's) the legs.

Pinto: (African term) a coffin.

Pissed-off: annoyed or angered.

Piss-poor: extremely poor in any respect.

Pistols: (1940's) zoot trousers.

Pitch a bitch: to complain; to fight; to cause noise.

Pitch a bull: (1940's) to have fun.

Plates: (1940's) the feet.

Platters: (1940's) the feet.

Play: (1930's-40's) a proposal; a scheme or plan.

Play dead: (1940's) to wait patiently.

Playing the dozens with one's uncle's cousin: (1940's) having the wrong approach to everything.

Play it cool: (1940's) unemotional, cautious, composed.

Plenty: (1900's-40's) good, excellent.

Pluck (plug): wine, especially cheap wine.

Plug the mug: (1940's) to stop talking.

Plumb: a very serious mistake.

Plunger: (1940's) a bathtub.

Poke: roll of money.

Poop out: (1930's-40's) to fail.

Pop: (1940's) to spend an excessive amount of money on someone in a social situation.

Poppa-stoppa: (1930's-40's) any old man who is effective at what he does.

Popper: (1940's) a gun.

Poppers: (1940's) fingers.

Pops: (1920's-30's) term of address by one male to another.

Pork chop (music): (1900's) a slow, barrelhouse style of jazz.

Portrait: (1940's) one's face.

Pot: marijuana.

Potato man: (1900's) a non-playing, instrument-carrying "musician" assigned to a 10- or 12-man marching band. His horn is plugged with potatoes.

Pot liquor: juice from greens; brew from marijuana seeds and stalks.

Pots (are) on: (1950's) in jazz, means the music is very beautiful and very effective.

Pounder: (1940's) a policeman or detective.

Pour man: (1940's) a bartender.

Power Dance (or Black Power Dance): the mood of reacting physically to oppression; looting.

Prat: to play coy (usually refers to a woman).

Prayer bones: (1920's-40's) the knees.

Prayer dukes: (1920's-40's) one's knees.

Prayer handles: (1920's-40's) the knees.

Press the flesh: to shake hands.

Pretty: (1900's) loosely used, in jazz, poor quality music.

Prez, Pres, President: Lester W. Young, 1909-1959, very famous tenor saxophonist.

Professor, prof: (1900's-30's) a pianist; an exceptionally learned person.

Promised land: Negro slave's concrete expression for the concept of freedom—usually referred to the northern states of the union, sometimes, to "Heaven."

Props: (1940's) legs, especially a girl's.

Puffed air: (1940's) having no food.

Pull (one's) coat: (1930's) to alert someone to something.

Pulleys: (1940's) suspenders.

Pumpkin: (1940's) the moon, or the sun.

Pump the stump: (1940's) to shake hands.

Punk: mostly midwest use for homosexual; in eastern states, a weak man.

Push: (1930's) to sell or distribute something (usually drugs).

Pusher: (1930's) one who delivers and sells narcotics.

Puss: (1940's) the face.

Pussy-whipped: to be henpecked or submerged by one's wife.

Put a spell on (someone): to work magic on a person.

Put-down: (1940's) to insult or reject someone.

Put (someone) in the alley: (1900's-20's) to play real soul music, down-home style.

Put on: original jazz use, to fake or tease or mislead.

Put (one) on: (1940's-70's) to ridicule a person who is not aware he or she is a victim of malicious fun.

Put on a crosstown bus: to deliberately confuse someone.

Put the issue on someone: (1940's) to give an inducted young man an army uniform, a gun and the required military training before sending him to the frontline.

Q

Queen: (1930's-40's) an attractive girl; (1950's) a male homosexual.

Quiet as it's kept: an expression used prior to revealing what is assumed to be a secret.

Quill: folded matchbook cover in which a narcotic is held and smoked or sniffed.

Quit it: to die.

Quit the scene: (1950's) to leave or to die.

R

Rabbit: John C. Hodges, born 1906, alto saxophonist; also, Richard Brown, born around 1880 in New Orleans, a country blues singer.

Race (music): (1920's-40's) the type of music generally known as Rhythm-and-Blues.

Racket-jacket: (1940's) a zoot suit.

Rag: (1940's) a magazine or newspaper.

Rag (music): (1890's-1920's) a distinct form of music that preceded jazz (or, as it has come to be known in the 1970's, "the sound of the black experience" or "the black experience in sound"), usually a very "hot" style.

Raghead: a black male who wears a scarf tied around his head to protect an expensive hairdo.

Ragmen: (1900's-20's) jazzmen who play that type of music.

Ragmop: messy, unkempt.

Rag out: (1860's-70's) to put on one's finest clothes.

Ragtime: (1890's-1920's) "hot" music that probably originated in Missouri; see *Rag (music)*.

Rain: used as a symbol of hard times.

Raise sand (cain): (1930's-40's) to make an outcry; to brawl; to fight; to stop.

Rank: (1920's-40's) faulty; to criticize; stupid flaw.

Rap: to hold conversation; a long, impressive monologue.

Rat hole: (1940's) one's pocket.

Raunchy: (1940's-50's) very bad, cheap in quality.

Ready: (1930's-40's, revived in 60's) hip; receptive.

Real: (1940's-60's) sincere, genuine.

Rebop: (1940's) a four-beat—early term for complex jazz.

Reckless eyeballing: looking with desire at "forbidden" persons; flirting.

Red: Henry Allen, Jr., born 1908, trumpeter and singer.

Red gravy: (1940's) blood.

Reefer: (1920's-50's) marijuana wrapped in cigarette paper.

Reefer man: (1920's-50's) one who sells marijuana; a pusher.

Reet: (1930's-40's) (from "right" in "all right") good, yes, excellent.

Rent party: (1920's-40's) a party given in one's home to make money to pay the rent; the guests pay for admission and for food and drinks.

Rep: reputation.

Repent pad: (1940's) a bachelor's apartment where a girl may be led to engage in an act she may later regret.

Rhythm-and-Blues (R and B): a relaxed style of singing and playing so ethnically oriented that it has little appeal to other groups (unless transformed so that it has a less "nitty-gritty" character).

Rib: (1940's) refers to a full, hot supper.

Ride man: (1920's-40's) in jazz, the leading soloist, who establishes the pace.

Ride out: (1920's) the playing of the last chorus in a jazz arrangement.

Ridiculous: (1930's) surprisingly delightful.

Riff: (1900's-40's) can refer to many things, ideas or situations; in jazz, it is often a quick ostinato melodic figure; also, to sing verbal sounds without intelligible meaning—popularized by Louis Armstrong and Ella Fitzgerald.

Righteous: (1900's-40's) authentic; correct.

Righteous moss: white folks' hair.

Right on: (1960) cry of approval; affirmation of a revolutionary spirit.

Rigor mortis (rig city, rigville): (1950's) a bad urban situation, especially in terms of finding employment.

Rind: (1940's) one's skin.

Ripped: (1950's) unhappy; in grief.

Ripper: (1940's) one who has a reputation for cutting others with a knife.

Roach: (1930's-60's) the butt of a reefer.

Rock: (1900's-30's) to dance; to have sexual intercourse; to sway to music; a type of swing music.

Rock candy: (1940's) diamonds.

Rockets: bullets.

Rockpile: (1940's) any tall building.

Roll: (1900's-40's) a rippling quality in music; a wad of paper money; to have sex.

Rommel: (1940's) to do an "about face," like the Nazi General.

Romp: (1900's-40's) to dance to music; to make gutbucket music.

Room: (1950's) bar or lounge.

Roost: (1940's-50's) where one lives; home.

Rooster: a man.

Rope: (1940's) a marijuana cigarette.

Roscoe: (1940's) a pistol (Southern Negro college student use).

Rosewood: a billystick, otherwise known as a policeman's nightstick.

Roust: to be harassed, especially by the police.

Rubber: (1930's-50's) a car.

Rubies: (1940's) one's lips (Southern Negro college student use).

Rudolph Hess: (1940's) to fade away.

Ruff: (1940's) a quarter.

Rugcutter: (1920's-30's) one who dances a lot, especially at parties; a good dancer.

Run away: (1900's) to be ahead of something or someone.

Run it down: to tell the whole truth of whatever is in question.

Run (one's) mouth: to talk excessively; to complain.

Running changes: (1920's-40's) in jazz, fast movement from one key change to another; also undergoing a number of emotional and psychological changes in a very short span.

Rusty dusty: (1940's-50's) the buttocks.

S

Safety: (1940's) one's bed.

Sails: (1940's) the ears.

Salty: to be irritated; ill-tempered; angry.

Sam: a Negro who conforms to ordinary patterns, from "Ol' Black Sam."

Sambo: any black American who accepts meekly his or her oppression; from "Little Black Sambo," a story with stereotypes that serve the purpose of false propaganda.

Same ol' same ol': a routine thing or situation.

Sand: (1930's-40's) a popular Harlem-oriented dance.

Sassy: (1930's-50's) term for a little girl who is disobedient; vibrating with youthful energy.

Satch, Satchmo: Daniel Louis Armstrong, born 1900, trumpeter, singer, band leader; famous and important jazz figure.

Satchel-mouth: person with a big mouth; "Satchmo," for Louis Armstrong, was the corruption of this term.

Saturday-night fish-fry: (1930's-40's) a very popular week-end social event in small Southern towns that did not survive very long in the urban environment.

Saw: landlord or lady of a cheap rooming house.

Sax: saxophone.

Saying something: speaking with profundity; refers to anything impressive or profound.

Scare: (1940's) a pleasant surprise.

Scarf: (1940's) to eat.

Scat: (1920's) generally attributed to Louis Armstrong, who, when he forgot the words of a song would make up syllables, often trying to imitate verbally the sounds of musical instruments; a kind of spontaneous "sound" poetry that may sound like "doubletalk" to unreceptive, white ears.

Scene: (1940's-50's) the main area of popular group activity, such as a street corner, a bar, a poolroom.

Scoff, scarf: (1930's-50's) to eat; see *Grease*.

Scoffing fishheads and scrambling for the gills: (1940's) having a very difficult time.

Score: (1930's-50's) to obtain something of value; a person whose compliance has been won.

Scrap iron: (1940's) bad liquor (Southern Negro college student use).

Scratch: money.

Scratch-crib: (1940's) a cheap hotel or rooming house—so called because the expected bedbug-bites cause one to scratch one's flesh.

Scream: (1930's) in jazz, a high-pitched trumpet sound; to complain about oppression and exploitation.

Screamer: (1930's) a jazzman who produces a scream-like effect through his trumpet.

Screaming fairy: a very obvious homosexual.

Screaming gasser: (1940's) police squad car or patrol wagon moving through traffic with its siren going full-blast.

Scribe: a letter.

Scrunch: (1900's-30's) a slow, dragged-out dance.

Scuffle: (1930's) difficulty; great hardship; a struggle.

Search me: (1940's) statement expressing innocence or ignorance.

Second line: (1900's) the line of children who playfully trailed the marching bands of parades or funerals (usually in New Orleans).

See: (1930's-40's) to read music.

Sell out to the Yankees: to move to a Northern industrial area.

Semolia: a fool.

Send: (1930's-40's) to arouse emotionally.

Sender: (1930's-40's) one who arouses emotionally; one who inspires excitement.

Set: in jazz, a working session, usually about 20 or 30 minutes.

Setup: to get ready; whiskey, ice, and chaser served in a barroom.

Sew: to perform autoerotism.

Shad: Lester Rallingston Collins; trumpeter, born in Elizabeth, N.J., 6-27-1910, played with Benny Carter and Cab Calloway.

Shades: (1950's) dark glasses.

Shafts: (1940's) one's legs.

Shag: (1900's) a fast jump dance; earthy; down-home.

Shake: (1920's) an Oriental dance style done in jazz terms; to dance exotically.

Shake (oneself) apart: (1900's-40's) to lose self-control either while dancing or laughing or crying.

Shake it, Shake that thing: (1900's-50's) to dance fast with great feeling.

Shake up: (1950's) to unsettle emotionally.

Shaking: (1950's) same as *Happening, example,* "What's shaking?"

Sharp: (1920's-40's) stylishly and attractively dressed.

Sheet: an official police record.

Shield: detective or police badge.

Shimmy: (1920's-40's) a dance, from the word "chemise." Women dancing at the Cotton Club in Harlem would shake their shoulders, and the part of their chemise that covered the breasts shook to the rhythm of their dancing bodies; thus the dance became known as the shimmy.

Shine: (1900's-30's) based upon a caste system psychology, a colored person who assumed that a black skin was ugly, would refer to a jet-black person as *shine; examples,* "He's so black he shines!" and, "I don't call you shine 'cause you mine!"

Shit: (1900's-50's) a word loosely used as an abbreviation for bullshit; stuff, nonsense; jive; personal affairs; drugs; whisky; conversation; almost anything.

Shiv: a switch blade knife; in prison, a homemade knife.

Shoe: a well-dressed person.

Shoeick: (1940's) one's feet.

Shoeshine-black: (1960's) the ideology of black consciousness.

Shoot em up: a western movie, the Hollywood type.

Shooting gravy: when an addict reinjects his own cooked blood.

Shooting the agate: (1900's) a kind of "hip" strut done in parades or often anywhere on the street in New Orleans and Memphis.

Shooting the marbles from all sides of the ring: (1940's) to be in a very dangerous position.

Short: (1940's) an automobile; see *Rubber*.

Short trill: (1940's) a short walk.

Shout: (1920's) the kind of hymn-singing that went on at revival meetings; a slow blues or spiritual done like a chant; gospel-singing.

Shouter: (1920's) a gospel singer or blues singer with a gospel orientation.

Showcase nigger: Negro hired by a white-owned firm to sit out front as a living example of the "fair" hiring practices of the company.

Showing out: (1890's) to flaunt one's self or one's possessions; to put on airs.

Shuck dropping: (1940's) taking advantage of an unsuspecting person.

Shucking and jiving: originally, Southern Negro expression for clowning, lying, pretense.

Shuffle: (1900's) a style of dancing and dance music done in 4/4 time, with 8 notes to a measure.

Shut eye: (1940's) sleep.

Shutters: (1940's) one's eyelids or eyes.

Sick: the feeling and discomfort of being without drugs when the craving is present.

Side(s): (1930's-50's) disk played on a phonograph machine.

Sideman: (1930's) any musician in a group other than the soloist; one's supporting friend in a situation.

Signify: same as the *Dirty Dozens;* to censure in 12 or fewer statements; see *Cap on.*

Silk: a white girl or woman; the reference is to her hair.

Sing: (1920's) in jazz, to make one's instrument sound lyrical.

Sister: a black woman, soul sister; female member of a Negro church; also, among black male homosexuals, a fellow homosexual.

Sit in: (1930's-50's) when a nonprofessional or outside musician is invited to join a working group on the stand in a public place; during the civil rights movement "sit-in" took on another meaning. In a dramatic attempt to break down the entrenched walls of public segregation, particularly in the South, black people and white liberals went in droves into restaurants and other public places where black people had been systematically rejected and staged a "sit-in."

Six: (1940's) grave.

Sizzle: to be dangerously subject to arrest, usually for the possession of illegal drugs.

Skate: (1940's) to escape paying a debt.

Skeeter: Clifton Best, guitarist, born in Kinston, N.C., 11-20-1914; worked with Kenny Clarke and Oscar Pettiford.

Skiffle (band): (1900's) a shuffle style of music or the group that makes it.

Skiffling and skuffling: (1940's) frantic activity.

Skillet: a black person.

Skin: the human hand; *example,* "Give me some skin!" To slap hands with someone, a friendly gesture, distinctly black, considered manly; (1920's-30's) drums.

Skin-beater: (1930's-40's) a drummer.

Skin-popping: taking drugs intramuscularly.

Skippy: a homosexual or effeminate man.

Skull-drag: any performance or task that taxes the mind heavily.

Sky: refers to the blue uniform of a law-enforcement officer; (1940's) a hat or a helmet.

Sky-piece: (1930's) a hat or cap.

Sky-pocket: (1940's) pocket inside one's outer garments, such as a vest pocket.

Slab: (1940's) bread.

Slam, slammer: (1930's) a jail.

Slanters: (1940's) one's eyes.

Slap: (1920's) to pluck the strings of a violin.

Slap-happy: (1940's) a devoted swing music fan.

Slat: sometimes refers to the length of a prison term or quantities of other things, such as money.

Slave: (1930's-40's) a job; to work; (1960's) an oppressed person; a drug addict.

Slave tip: (1940's) a lead on a job.

Slay (one): (1940's) a request to be told stunning news.

Slicing (one's) chops: (1940's) talking.

Slick: an underhanded person; the "art" of being clever.

Slide: Locksley Wellington Hampton, trombonist, composer, born in Jeannette, Pa., 4-21-1932; worked with Lionel Hampton; (1920's) a glissando way of playing the piano.

Slide (one's) jib: (1940's) to talk.

Slides: (1930's-40's) shoes.

Sliphorn: (1900's-40's) trombone.

Slipstick: trombone.

Slops and slugs: (1940's) coffee and doughnuts.

Slum hustler: one who peddles cheap costume jewelry.

Slurp: glissando piano style.

Smack: James Fletcher Henderson, 1898-1952, band leader, composer, pianist; also, heroin.

Small pipe: alto sax.

Smart stuff: tricky; underhanded activity.

Smarty-pants: boy who has begun to feel mature sexual desire.

Smashed: drunk.

Smear: (1920's) in jazz, a slightly flat tonal quality.

Smit smoke: (1940's) a very intelligent black person.

Smoke (them) out: (1950's) to be really fantastic, especially in making good music; see *Cook*.

Smokes: cigarettes.

Smoke screen: (1940's) under-arm deodorant.

Smooth: very adept; clever.

Snake: a sneaky person.

Snake doctor: dragonfly.

Snake Hips: (1900's-30's) a Baltimore- and New York-oriented jazz dance.

Snap: to move fast.

Snap a snapper: (1940's) to light a match.

Snapper: (1940's) a wooden match.

Snatch: the vagina; female sexuality.

Snatcher: (1930's) policeman.

Sneezer: (1940's) a handkerchief.

Sniff a powder: (1940's) to run away or leave.

Sniffer: (1940's) one's nose.

Snip a dolly: (1940's) to go away.

Snipe: (1940's) a cigarette or cigar stub.

Snitch: to inform against someone.

Snitcher: (1940's) a newspaper reporter.

Snitch-sheet: (1940's) a newspaper.

Snort: to inhale drugs.

Snuffer: (1940's) one's nose.

Sock: originally, a drummer's double cymbals; also, to hit, move fast, to inform; *example*, "Sock it to me!"

Sock frock: (1940's) one's best suit.

Soft-top: (1940's) a stool.

Soft touch: easily victimized person.

Solid: (1930's-60's) describes a fine state of affairs; anything marvelous or truly great; loyal; trustworthy.

Solid sender: a very "together" and satisfying person.

Solitaire: (1940's) suicide.

Some lip: talking back in self-defense; see *Lip.*

Some pig: talk; conversation.

Some skin: hand-slap greeting; see *Skin.*

Something else: (1950's-60's) any extraordinary person, place, thing or idea.

Sometimey: (1940's-50's) possessing a very changeable personality.

Sonny: Theodore W. Rollins, born 1929; famous tenor saxophonist.

Soul: the sensitivity and emotional essence that derives from the blues; the heritage that is black; a natural process; black authenticity; feeling for one's roots, as demonstrated in black music and literature.

Soul brother: one black man to another; see *Blood brother.*

Soul City: Harlem.

Soul food: Southern-style cooking done by black Americans; see *Blackplate, Chit'lins, Corn bread, Cow pea soup, Crackling biscuit, Dumplings, Ham-bone soup.*

Soul on: phrase of encouragement to one to continue to be authentic.

Soul sister: a black girl or woman.

Sound: (1940's-50's) point of view; *example,* "How you sound?"

Sounding (on a chick): flirting.

Sounds: (1940's) music, especially jazz.

Spade: (1940's-50's) a Negro (probably picked up from white usage).

Spare: (1940's) a friend.

Spark: (1940's) a match, cigarette or a diamond.

Spasm band: (1900's) a group of musicians who get together with homemade instruments and form a marching band.

Speaker: a gun.

Speedball: injection of cocaine and heroin mixed.

Spiel: (1940's) to talk, especially for a long time.

Spilling: older term that means same as "rapping"—talking.

Spin a hen: (1940's) to dance with an older woman.

Spinning at the track on fool's dim: (1940's) to go dancing with a girl (who works as a maid) on her night off.

Splap: a variant pronunciation of "slap."

Splash: (1940's) a bath.

Split: (1950's-70's) to leave.

Spook: (1940's) a Negro (picked up from white usage).

Spot: (1900's) usually a nightclub but also any popular place.

Spots: (1920's) music symbols on sheet music.

Spotters: (1940's) one's eyes.

Spouting: (1940's) excessive talking.

Square: (1920's-60's) orthodox person, one who supports popular mainstream values; a conventional person; unenlightened; innocent.

Squaresville: a place dominated by squares.

Square up: to leave the scene and start a new life along more conventional lines.

Squat: (1940's) to sit down.

Squatpad: (1940's) a lounge or lobby.

Squatter: (1940's) a stool or chair.

Squeal: to inform against someone.

Squeeze: a difficult situation; a belt.

Stable: a big-time pimp's prostitutes.

Stacked: refers to a well-shaped woman's body.

Stag: a detective.

Stagger Lee: a character in Negro folklore. He accuses someone called Billy of cheating at dice, goes home and returns with his gun. At gun-point, Billy begs for his life to no avail; not only is Billy shot but the bullet passes through his body and breaks the bartender's glass. In other words, Stagger Lee is an angry nigger.

Stallion: a good-looking black woman (a matriarchal implication?); see *Cock*.

Stand tall: go forth with pride; to be ready for any occasion.

Stand up: to show remarkable strength, a capacity for survival under poor odds; *example*, "Black people in the United States are *stand-up* people!"

Stash: (1930's-60's) to hide booty, drugs or liquor.

Steal away: escape.

Stealers: (1940's) the fingers.

Steel: (rare) white Anglo-Saxon person.

Stems: (1940's) the legs.

Stepinfetchit: an Uncle Tom, a slave, a Sambo (derived from a Negro Hollywood character actor and the subservient roles he played).

Step-off: (1940's) a street curb.

Stewer: (1940's) an old woman.

Stewie: (1940's) a drunk.

Stick: (1920's-40's) a reefer or a clarinet.

Sticks: (1900's) drumsticks.

Stick-up man: one who performs armed robbery.

Stiffing and jiving: (1930's-40's) an impressive showing but with little actual substance.

Stiffing the stroll: (1940's) act of standing on the corner.

Stilts: (1940's) the legs.

Sting: to rob; also refers to booty gained from a robbery.

Stingy brim: narrow-brimmed hat.

Stinky-pie rich: very wealthy.

Stir: (1940's) jail.

Stomp: (1900's-50's) a heavy-footed, action-packed dance; a jazz instrumental competition; to beat someone, to kick, stamp under the feet.

Stompers: (1940's) one's shoes or feet.

Stomp off: (1900's) a foot-rhythm signal used by musicians to correlate the starting of their performance.

Stomps: (1940's) one's shoes.

Stone: a greater degree of anything; precise; also, an intensifying prefix.

Stoned: (1940's-70's) ecstatic; see *High*.

Stone fox: a beautiful black girl or woman.

Stone soul: great soul.

Stooling: (1940's) informing on someone—especially one black person informing on another to a white authority-figure.

Story: (1930's-50's) a person's problems, but especially an explanation or an excuse.

Storyville: (1896-1917) the district in New Orleans commonly credited as the birthplace of formal jazz. It was an area where whorehouses were openly and legally maintained and where black musicians could actually find employment.

Straight: (1930's-60's) a good feeling; to be above suspicion; to feel especially well after taking drugs; without exaggeration; heterosexual.

Straighten: (1930's-60's) to straighten someone is to tell her or him the truth or to pay back money borrowed.

Straps: (1930's-40's) suspenders.

Streamer issue: (1930's-40's) necktie.

Street: among prisoners, the world beyond prison walls; (1920's-50's) road. The habit of referring to a city street as a road was probably left over from the black rural experience.

Street Arabs: the more orthodox robe-wearing Moslems of Harlem.

Streevus mone on the reevus cone: a jitterbug expression that has no specific meaning.

Stretch: a prison sentence.

Stretcher: (1930's-40's) a belt, suspenders or a necktie.

Stretch out: (1950's-60's) to operate without false restraint; to explore; to be uninhibited.

Striders: (1940's) trousers.

Strides: (1940's) trousers.

Striding: (1930's-40's) in jazz, playing a ten-key stretch in bass on a piano.

Strike and fade!: (1960's) commit the deed, then vanish (slogan used as instruction for those working in the "organized" area of a riot).

Stroll: (1930's-40's) any easy commitment; a road or street.

Struggle: (1900's-30's) in jazz, a bad performance; (1960's), short for the Civil Rights struggle.

Struggle buggy: (1930's-40's) a very old rundown car.

Strung out: (1950's-60's) addicted, especially to a heavy drug.

Strut, strutter, strut one's stuff: (1900's-30's) a fancy-step slow dance; one who does the dance.

Stud: a hip male (without the white sexual connotation).

Stud-hoss: (1930's-40's) usually rural usage, a term of greeting by one male to another. (The reference is probably white in origin.)

Stud with many fingers: (1940's) J. Edgar Hoover and his Federal Bureau of Investigation agents.

Stuff: Hezekiah Leroy Gordon Smith, singer and songwriter, born in Portsmouth, Ohio, 8-14-1909; worked with Dizzy Gillespie among others; (1920's-40's) jive; drugs; almost anything.

Stumble: (1940's) to encounter serious misfortune.

Suckass: servile; a flunky.

Suffering with the shorts: (1940's) to be without money.

Sugar: a kiss.

Sugar Hill: a whorehouse district in a black community; also, in Harlem, a very popular middle-class neighborhood.

Suitcase: (1930's-40's) drums.

Sunday-go-to-the-meeting clothes: one's best-looking, finest garments.

Sunny side (of the street): the "good life"; luxury, leisure and comfort.

Superspade: a black person who is extremely racially self-conscious. (The term may be of white origin and picked up by blacks.)

Susie (Suzie, Suzy): (1930's-40's) a Cotton Club original jazz dance.

Swabble: to gulp food (probably a variation of gobble).

Swag: stolen goods.

Sweat: (1950's-60's) to be nervous, upset.

Sweet: (1920's-40's) the white musician's interpretation of jazz; the type of music played by Paul Whiteman and Benny Goodman.

Sweet mama: black female lover.

Sweet man: black male lover.

Sweet papa: a sugar-daddy and sweet man.

Sweets: Harry Edison, trumpeter, born in Columbus, Ohio, 10-10-1915; worked with Count Basie and Josephine Baker; jazz-man.

Sweet tooth: having a craving for sweets.

Swing: (1930's) a style of white music that developed from hot jazz; also, a type of black music developed by Duke Ellington; (1950's) to have fun, to give pleasure.

Swinger: (1950's) originally a very thrilling musician; anyone who goes all-out to have a good time; a professional pleasure-seeker.

Swinging: (1950's) an expression of approval.

Swing like a rusty gate: a *good* performance of swing music (derogatory).

Swish: to flaunt homosexual characteristics or what are thought to be such; to flaunt the body.

Switch: (1940's) short for switchblade knife.

Swith: (1940's-50's) to smell.

Swoop: to go, leave; see *Split*.

Swopping slop: (1940's) kissing (Southern Negro college student use).

Sylvester: a white man; see *Mister Charlie*.

T

Tab action: (1940's) to borrow something, especially money.

Tab issue: (1940's) the business of borrowing.

Tabs: (1940's) one's ears.

Tacky: ill-composed.

Tag: (1920's) in jazz, a footnote-like musical phrase at the end of a chorus.

Tagged the play with the slammer issue: (1940's) the act of putting a troublesome person in jail.

Take: (1920's-30's) in show business, payment for work done; the amount of money earned by a group effort.

Take a leak: to urinate.

Take a powder: (1940's) to leave. (Obviously picked up from white use, probably the movies.)

Take care of business (TCB): (1950's-70's) to meet one's commitments with efficiency; to perform effectively, skillfully.

Take it slow (easy): (1930's-40's) said in farewell to someone.

Take off: (1930's-50's) to experiment; to do something different; also to rob or hurt.

Take to the cleaners: to rob, strip someone.

Talk: (1920's-40's) when a jazzman is really communicating through his music people often cry out "Talk to me!" Or they might say, "He's saying something!"

Talking trash: to jive, pretend, lie.

Tall money: a great deal of wealth.

Tape: (1950's) to control with understanding.

113

Taste: (1940's-60's) liquor usually, but also any small amount of anything.

Taters: potatoes, a principal soul food staple.

Tattler: (1940's) an alarm clock.

Tea: (1920's) marijuana.

Tea pad: (1920's-30's) a place where one can purchase and smoke marijuana.

Tear out: (1900's-50's) to move fast.

Tears: (1940's) pearls.

Tear (it) up: (1920's-1940's) in jazz, to give a great performance.

Teed: (1940's) drunk.

Tell a story: see *Talk, Story*.

Tell it like it is: see *Like it is*.

Ten: (1940's) one's toes.

Ten bones: (1940's) the fingers of both hands.

Terrible: (1950's-60's) to be really wonderful, great.

Testify: to confess one's sins, bad deeds, life story (originally in church but now also in music, in literature and through other forms of art).

Texas Shuffle: a 1938 Count Basie recording; good Basie stride.

There you go!: (1930's-50's) an expression of assent.

Thing, one's own: (1950's-70's) a personal way of doing something; an individual's life style, ideas, or career.

Thinkbox: (1930's-40's) one's head, brain, mind.

Thinkpad: (1940's) the mind.

Thin one: (1930's-40's) a dime.

Third stream: a type of music (by people like Charlie Mingus and John Lewis) that reflects to a very noticeable degree both the European and black technical experience.

Threads: (1930's) one's garments, especially a suit.

Three-pointer: (1940's) a corner; *example*, "Three-pointer of the ace trill in the twirling top"—any busy corner of Seventh Avenue in Harlem; a corner on the main street.

Tick: (1930's-40's) a minute.

Tick-tock: (1940's) the heart-beat.

Ticky: (1930's-40's) old-fashioned, stiff, mechanical, stale.

Timber: (1940's) a toothpick.

Tinkler: (1930's-40's) a bell, such as a doorbell.

Tip out: to have sex with someone other than one's spouse.

Tipple: (1920's-30's) stringed ukulele.

Toddle: (1920's-30's) slow jazz tempo and dance.

Tog: (1920's) to dress fashionably and expensively.

Together: (1950's-70's) to have one's mind free of confusion; to be positive, functional; to emerge as a whole person; see *Down*.

Togged to the bricks: dressed extremely well.

Togs: (1920's) clothing.

Tom: see *Uncle Tom*.

Tomcat: a well-dressed dude who is out searching for a willing sexual companion.

Tony: stylish and snobbish.

Too much: (1930's-60's) a phrase connoting high praise; something inscrutable.

Tooth booth: (1940's) a dentist's office (Southern Negro college student use).

Tooting stomps: (1940's) low-quarter shoes.

Top: (1930's-40's) the end; to be in front.

Top-flat: (1940's) one's head.

Top Sergeant: (1940's) a lesbian.

Topside of the rockpile: (1940's) the top floor of an apartment building.

Tore up: (1950's) drunk; unhappy.

Torn down: distressed.

Tough: (1950's) great, wonderful; difficult, terrible.

Tough shit: bad luck; difficulty.

Tough titty: hard luck ("tough titty but the milk is good!").

Tower of Pisa: (1940's) leaning or to lean.

Toy band: (1930's-40's) a group of musicians who produce popular, synthetic sounds.

Track: (1930's-40's) a ballroom or dance hall; a musical piece on a phonograph record.

Tracks: marks and scars on the arm or other areas of the body from hypodermic injections of heroin.

Trade: sexual customers for a prostitute or homosexual.

Trane: John William Coltrane, tenor saxophonist, born in Hamlet, North Carolina, 9-23-26; a highly original musician and one of the greatest jazz figures of all times.

Trap: (1940's) the military draft board.

Traps: trapdrums.

Treaders: (1940's) shoes.

Tree-suit: (1940's) coffin.

Trey of sous: (1940's) three nickels.

Trey of sous and a double ruff: (1940's) forty cents.

Trick: a prostitute's customer or the transaction itself.

Trickeration: (1940's) to show off; flaunting one's self or objects of pride.

Trig (one's) wig: (1940's) to think fast.

Trill: (1930's) a fancy way of walking.

Trim: a woman's sexuality; to have sex with a woman.

Triple-hip: extremely wise.

Trip (one) out: to get extremely high ("stoned") either on drugs or an idea or situation.

Trods: (1940's) one's feet.

Trotters: pig's feet; (1940's) one's legs.

Truck: (1900's-40's) go, walk, dance.

Truck driver: (homosexual use) extremely masculine homosexual.

Trucking: (1930's) a dance introduced in Harlem's famous Cotton Club.

Trummy: James Osborne Young, born 1912; trombonist and singer.

Trump the hump: (1940's) climb the hill.

Truth: (1940's) good, authentic jazz, played with great feeling.

Tube: (1940's) the New York City subway; (1960's) a television set.

Tubs: (1930's) drums.

Tune: (1940's) (very loosely used) an idea or a woman.

Tuned in: in rapport with whatever is going on; the opposite is "tuned out."

Tune in our mikes: (1940's) to listen.

Turf: the street one lives on (mainly in New York City).

Turkey Trot: (1900's-20's) a jazz dance.

Turned on: a high degree of response.

Turn on: get high; to give or sell drugs to someone; to give someone advice.

Turn out: to initiate a beginner to the scene—drugs or whatever else is currently fashionable.

Turtles: (1940's) body turns.

Tush: a wealthy, light-skinned society Negro.

Tushroon: money.

Twig: (1930's-40's) a tree.

Twilight world: the world of all-night parties.

Twinkle: (1940's) a doorbell, the sound it makes.

Twisted: (1950's) to be intoxicated.

Twister: doorkey.

Two camels: (1940's) ten minutes.

Two cents: (1940's) two dollars.

Two-story lorry: (1940's) a doubledecker bus.

U

Ugly as homemade sin: an abusive remark.

Ultracool: a high level of hipness and togetherness.

Uncle: (1940's) a pawnshop manager.

Uncle Ben black: a deep sense of black racial consciousness.

Uncle Sam's action: (1940's) induction into military service.

Uncle Sham: a derogatory variant of Uncle Sam.

Uncle Tom: a servile Negro (originally a character in the novel, *Uncle Tom's Cabin* by Harriet Beecher Stowe); the creation of Bop (in the 1940's) was a rebellion on the part of young black musicians to the "Uncle Tom" music that preceded it.

Uncool: (1950's) the opposite of *Cool.*

Unhip: (1950's) the opposite of *Hip.*

Unnecessary: describes a dejected feeling; *example,* "I feel so unnecessary."

Up: high.

Up against the wall, motherfucker: a popular phrase from the poem "Black People" by LeRoi Jones; name of a militant group.

Uppity: arrogant; sophisticated.

Uprights: (1940's) one's legs.

Ups: stimulant drugs.

Up South: the phrase implying that racial bigotry in the North is no less vicious than in the South.

Upstairs: (1930's-40's) the Christian concept of Heaven in the sky.

Up-tempo: (1930's) fast tempo music.

Uptight: song sung by Stevie Wonder; a good feeling; a bad feeling; anxiety; under strain.

Uptown: stylishness; wealth.

V

Vacuum cleaner: (1940's) one's lungs.

V-8: (1940's) an unfriendly female.

Vibes: (1930's) short for vibraphone, vibraharp and vibrabells.

Vic: a victim.

Ville: (1940's) popular suffix often attached to any word as an intensifier.

Vine: (1930's) a suit of clothing.

Viper: (1920's-40's) drug dealer.

W

Waders: (1940's) boots.

Wail: (1950's) a truly beautiful delivery, especially in the performance of music.

Walk: (1950's) in jazz, four-beats-to-the-bar rhythm.

Walk-back: (1930's-40's) a rear apartment.

Walk-down: (1940's) a basement apartment.

Walk heavy: carry oneself in a self-glorifying manner.

Walking bass: (1900's-40's) in jazz, whole bass tones, broken octaves, a progression with an up-and-down movement of semitones.

Walking the dog: (1916-20) a popular jazz dance.

Waller: (1950's) an expert pianist but also any musician who is a true artist (from Thomas "Fats" Waller, 1904-1943, pianist, singer, and songwriter).

Washboard band: (1900's-30's) a group of jazzmen utilizing washboards (by rubbing their fingers or thimbles over the surfaces) as musical instruments.

Washer: (1940's) a tavern.

Waste: (1950's) to murder or injure someone.

Waters: (1940's) boots.

Waterworks: (1940's) tears.

Way out: (1950's) extreme, usually positive.

Wear a smile: (1940's) to be naked.

Weed: (1920's-40's) marijuana; (1940's) to lend someone something, especially money.

Weight: one's influence; see *Heavy*.

121

Weird: (1940's-60's) refers to a surprise and sometimes to a delightful surprise.

Weirdie, weird-o: (1950's) an unusual person.

Wet one's whistle: to take a drink, especially liquor.

Whale: to throw dice or to be very active in some other gambling activity; to do anything very effectively.

What's cooking(?): (1930's-40's) what's going on?

What's your song King Kong?: (1940's) how do you feel?

Wheelchair: (1940's) an automobile.

Wheels: (1930's) a car.

Where (one) is at: (1960's) one's essential nature or central philosophy.

Whing-ding: a boisterous party.

Whip out: to show, do, expose, give.

Whipped up: (1930's-40's) physically beaten; exhausted.

White house: white society.

White lilies: (1940's) bed sheets.

White Negro (nigger): a Negro with white affectations; a white person with Negro affectations.

Whitey: the white man.

Whore scars: needle-marks on the skin; see *Tracks.*

Whup: (1940's) hangover (Southern Negro college student use).

Wig: (1930's-50's) a man's or woman's natural hair that has been processed or straightened; one's mentality, brain, skull, thoughts.

Wigged out: see *Twisted.*

Wigglers: (1940's) fingers.

Wiggy: pleasing, especially when referring to a condition.

Wig out: to excite or thrill.

Wild: (1940's-60's) deeply satisfying.

Willie The Lion: William Henry Joseph Berthol Bonaparte Berlholoff Smith, pianist and composer; born 1897 in Goshen, N. Y.

Willy: a house nigger; see *Field nigger.*

Windbags: (1940's) one's lungs.

Wind pumps: (1940's) lungs.

Windy City: (1940's) Chicago.

Wishbone: a forked chickenbone held and broken by two persons making a silent wish; the one who breaks off the larger portion will have his wish fulfilled.

With it (be or get): (1940's-50's) to have rapport with whatever is happening.

Wolf: an extremely aggressive male heterosexual or homosexual.

Wolverine: (1940's) a female flirt.

Woodpile: (1930's-40's) xylophone.

Woodshed: (1930's) in jazz, when a musician practices his instrument in privacy.

Work: (1940's) sexual activity; (1950's) in jazz, to play with great energy.

Worm: to study.

Wow!: (1950's-70's) an expression of delightful surprise or simple astonishment.

Wren: (1940's) a young woman or girl.

Wringling and twisting: (1940's) discrimination and segregation.

Writer: (1920's-30's) one who writes songs or music.

Wrong: (1950's) defective quality.

Wrong riff: (1930's-40's) anything out of order; a mistake. (Originally a jazz term but took on general black usage.)

Wrong side of the tracks: an undesirable community.

X

X'ed out: something formerly important that is no longer significant.

Y

Yacky-yack: originally, "yack" meant a stupid person but later referred to a stupid conversation.

Yam: (1940's) to eat.

Yardbird: Charlie Parker or Charles Christopher Parker, Jr., alto saxophonist, born in Kansas City, Kansas, 8-29-1920 and died in New York City, 3-12-1955; see *Bird*.

Yarddog: (1940's) a dumb person.

Yeah: (1950's) an exclamation expressing approval.

Yeasting: to exaggerate (since yeast is what makes bread rise).

Yellow eye: (1940's) an egg.

Yellow girl: (1860's) a light-skinned Negro female.

Yellow jacket: a yellow capsule containing a depressant drug.

Yoke: (1940's) a jitterbug collar.

Yola: (1940's) a light-complexioned Negro girl (Southern Negro college student use).

You know: a question-like interjection after a phrase or sentence.

Your (yo) bad self: addressed to one who has accomplished a remarkable act or piece of work. Bad, of course, means good; see *Bad*.

Your own thing: see *Thing*.

Yo yo: a dumb person, victim of routine; someone who is manipulated.

Z

Zanzy: (1940's-50's) realistic and excellent.

Zap: to move quickly.

Zazzle: sexual desire or exaggerated sensuousness.

Ziggerboo: (1940's) a crazy person (Southern Negro college student use).

Zonked: intoxicated, drunk, stoned, high.

Zoom: (1940's) to obtain something without paying for it; to sneak (without paying) into a public place (like a theater) where admission is charged.

Zoot: (1920's-40's) a fashionable and flashy style in clothing. Zoot suits have huge padded shoulders, zippered narrow cuffs, very fancy lapels and they expand at the knees.

Zoot suit action: (1940's) the competitive game of one zoot suit wearer trying to outdress the next zoot-decked person.